MW01065306

Prairie Flavors

[CELEBRATING 65 YEARS OF OKLAHOMA COOKING]

1948  2013

Prairie Flavors

[CELEBRATING 65 YEARS OF OKLAHOMA COOKING]

1948  2013

Edited by Laura Araujo

DEDICATION

This cookbook is dedicated to the consumer-members of Oklahoma's rural electric cooperatives.

THE
DONNING COMPANY
PUBLISHERS

The Donning Company Publishers
184 Business Park Drive, Suite 206
Virginia Beach, VA 23462

Steve Mull, *General Manager*
Barbara Buchanan, *Office Manager*
Heather L. Floyd, *Editor*
Stephanie Danko, *Graphic Designer*
Kathy Adams, *Imaging Artist*
Cindy Smith, *Project Research Coordinator*
Tonya Washam, *Marketing Specialist*
Pamela Engelhard, *Marketing Advisor*

Ed Williams, *Project Director*

Library of Congress Cataloging-in-Publication Data

Prairie flavors : celebrating 65 years of Oklahoma cooking, 1948-2013 / edited by Laura Araujo.
pages cm
Summary: Sixty-fifth-anniversary cookbook featuring recipes from the first issue of Oklahoma rural news (1948) to today's Oklahoma living magazine.
Includes index.
ISBN 978-1-57864-839-9 (hardcover : alkaline paper)
1. Cooking—Oklahoma. 2. Cooking, American. I. Araujo, Laura, 1981- II. Oklahoma rural news. III. Oklahoma living.
TX715.P897 2013
641.59766—dc23

2013029457

Printed in the United States of America at Walsworth Publishing Company

Unless noted, all photos used are from the *Oklahoma Living/Oklahoma Rural News* archives

Contents

Foreword 6
By Sid Sperry

Acknowledgments 7
By Laura Araujo

Introduction 8

Index 186

Breakfast & Brunch 12

Breads, Biscuits, & Muffins 28

Appetizers 46

Soups, Chilis, & Stews 62

Salads 76

Sides 88

Main Dishes & Casseroles 104

Around the World 132

Beverages 144

Desserts 158

Foreword

Beginning with the very first issue of the *Oklahoma Rural News*, which was first published in January 1948, there was an emphasis placed on educating farm families about making better and more profitable use of electricity in their homes and on their farms. These initial promotional efforts were led by the legendary Dr. Henry G. Bennett, then president of Oklahoma A&M College (now known as Oklahoma State University) in Stillwater, Oklahoma.

Dr. Bennett and Shawnee Brown, then the director of Extension Service at Oklahoma A&M College, requested that the Oklahoma Association of Electric Cooperatives (OAEC) name a committee to work with the college to produce outreach programs that promoted the safe and efficient use of electricity in rural homesteads. The programs not only educated rural citizens about light, but also served to enlighten housewives and homemakers about the many ways electricity could be put to good use through a vast array of new consumer products.

What started as the "Homemaker's Page" in the first issue of the *Oklahoma Rural News* has evolved into one of the most popular sections of today's *Oklahoma Living* magazine: our "Prairie Flavors" recipes page, which features wholesome and easy-to-make meals that receive rave reviews from loyal readers.

It is that kind of interaction with our readers that led our *Oklahoma Living* magazine staff to publish this sixty-fifth-anniversary cookbook, entitled *Prairie Flavors: Celebrating 65 Years of Oklahoma Cooking, 1948–2013.*

From hearty breakfast dishes to savory soups, this commemorative cookbook is filled with the best reader-submitted recipes we think you could ever find. Though cooking methods and kitchen appliances have changed through the years, the one common denominator that can be found in each and every recipe contained in this cookbook is the joy and love of living in rural Oklahoma as expressed by our readers. For that, we are forever grateful.

A farmer giving witness in a rural Tennessee church in the early 1940s said it best: "Brothers and sisters, I want to tell you this. The greatest thing on earth is to have the love of God in your heart, and the next greatest thing is to have electricity in your house."

We couldn't agree more.

In closing, it is with deep appreciation and gratitude that I extend a special "Thank You" to the writer and producer of this commemorative cookbook. Laura Araujo—an excellent cook and food specialist in her own right—has done an outstanding job in preparing this collection of both time-tested and new, innovative dishes. Laura has spent countless hours researching the archives of both the *Oklahoma Rural News* and *Oklahoma Living* magazine. Her love of blending personal stories into each and every recipe is evident in this wonderful collection.

Thank you, Laura, for making the recipes and the foods we eat more meaningful. This book would not have been possible without your tireless commitment and dedication to the "prairie flavors" of Oklahoma.

Sid Sperry
Director of Public Relations, Communications and Research
Oklahoma Association of Electric Cooperatives

Acknowledgments

Celebrations usually involve food. No matter where in Oklahoma you are or what the occasion celebrated might be, chances are there will be food. As *Oklahoma Living* magazine celebrates sixty-five years in 2013, it is fitting that we mark the occasion with food—a collection of decades of Oklahoma's best recipes.

As we celebrate, I would like to thank our dedicated readers. Your stories have made *Oklahoma Living* magazine what it is each month for the past sixty-five years. Likewise, you have made this cookbook what it is. In submitting your recipes, you have not only shared lists of ingredients and instructions for preparing food; you have shared your stories. The recipes are accounts of your grandparents and parents, joyful memories of the past, and special times spent with family and friends. I have truly enjoyed reading each one of them. Thank you for sharing them with all of us.

I am grateful to the Cherokee Nation for allowing us to use several of their recipes throughout the cookbook. Native Americans play a vital role in Oklahoma's history. Their recipes have enriched the cookbook and made it more representative of our great state.

To the cooperative communicators across Oklahoma, thank you for your support of the cookbook—for promoting it in your newsletters and for sharing personal recipes as well. I am proud that the cookbook represents the entirety of the state, featuring recipes from the members and staff of all twenty-eight of Oklahoma's distribution cooperatives as well as the two generation and transmission cooperatives. You have made this possible.

It has been a joy working with Heather Floyd, Stephanie Danko, Kathy Adams, Tonya Washam, and Ed Williams at The Donning Company Publishers. Thank you for answering my many questions and for making the cookbook publishing process go so smoothly.

Thank you to Sid Sperry for your vision and leadership in publishing the cookbook. The cookbook is the result of the vision of Anna Politano, who came up with this special way to celebrate sixty-five years of *Oklahoma Living* magazine. I can't think of a better way to commemorate the occasion. Thank you for your leadership and support. Thank you to Hayley Leatherwood for the technical support you provided, from your work with the website to designing ads and promoting the cookbook on social media. I appreciate all you have done behind the scenes to make the cookbook successful. Thank you to Christy Johnson and Kirbi Mills for your administrative support. And finally, I am grateful to our dedicated interns, Meg McElhaney and Kaylan Watkins, for your help with anything and everything, your creative ideas, and your willingness to dig through sixty-five years of dusty archives to make the cookbook a true representation of *Oklahoma Living*'s history.

Now that I have given thanks, let's dig in!

Laura Araujo
Editor

Introduction

The very first edition of the *Oklahoma Rural News* (now *Oklahoma Living* magazine) was published in January 1948. Clarence Reeds, then president of the Oklahoma Association of Electric Cooperatives (OAEC), wrote in his editorial that month, "Since 1943, the need has been felt for a publication which would serve as the voice of the thousands of cooperative members who had banded together locally to serve themselves electricity, and through their respective cooperatives, into a state organization to advance the program until every farmstead in Oklahoma has high-line service."

Sixty-five years later, electricity has made its way into most parts of rural Oklahoma, but *Oklahoma Living* magazine continues to move forward with its founding purpose at the core: "In each issue will be found national and state news of the rural electrification program; helpful information to enable farmers and their wives to make the best and most profitable use of electricity; and editorial comment to guide its readers in interpreting important events reported," Reeds wrote.

Though *Oklahoma Living*'s audience has changed through the years—readers live and work both in rural and urban areas—the magazine's objective is unchanged. In the year of 2013, *Oklahoma Living* celebrates sixty-five years of fulfilling this purpose.

More Power to Oklahoma Cooking

When lights first switched on in rural Oklahoma in December 1936, it changed everything—including the way people cooked and what people ate. Over the next several years, pioneers worked hard to electrify Oklahoma farms, an effort that forever raised the standard of living—and cooking—in the Oklahoma countryside.

In the charter edition of the *Oklahoma Rural News*, OAEC President Reeds wrote about the importance of electricity in raising the standard of cooking. "Women especially will find the *Oklahoma Rural News* of greatest benefit if they will read the 'Homemaker's Page'... Of all the countless benefits of electricity to the farm, nothing it does is more significant than that of raising the standard of living of those it serves. It is in this important phase of the program that women will play the most prominent role."

Oklahoma Rural News

Publication of Oklahoma Statewide REA Electric Cooperative

VOL. 1, NO. 2. FEBRUARY—1948 EIGHT PAGES

CONGRESSMAN JOHNSON TELLS CO-OP MANAGER HE IS FRIEND OF REA

Farmers' Friend

Joe C. Scott

55 WIRING INSPECTORS IN ATTENDANCE AT TWO REA-SPONSORED SCHOOLS

State PMA Committee Asks Statewide Association For Closer Cooperation

Farmers Union To Seek New Cabinet Post; Train Youth

Describes Invitation As "Grass Roots" Plan To Boost Agriculture

Over 100 Oklahomans To Attend National Co-op Convention In Chicago

Three Sooners Asked To Take Part In Program At NRECA Annual Meeting

Statewide Convention Postponed To April 21; To Be In Oklahoma City

Co-ops Pledge Support of SPA As Vital Power Supply Source

Oppose Thomas Bill And Others Seeking To Sell Power At Gov't Projects

Leaders At Wichita Conference

$360,000 Loan Approved For Caddo Electric Cooperative

Statewide Association Joins Agricultural Co-op Council

Co-op Officials Discuss REA Plan With Farm Bureau Board

One of the first editions of the Oklahoma Rural News, *printed in February 1948.*

Previous to electricity, preparing meals was an arduous task; there was no "ding" of the microwave after the push of a button and a five-minute countdown to dinner. Water had to be hauled inside since there was no electric pump to feed the house. Logs had to be chopped to fuel the wood stove. A smoky oil lamp lighted the kitchen in the absence of electric lighting.

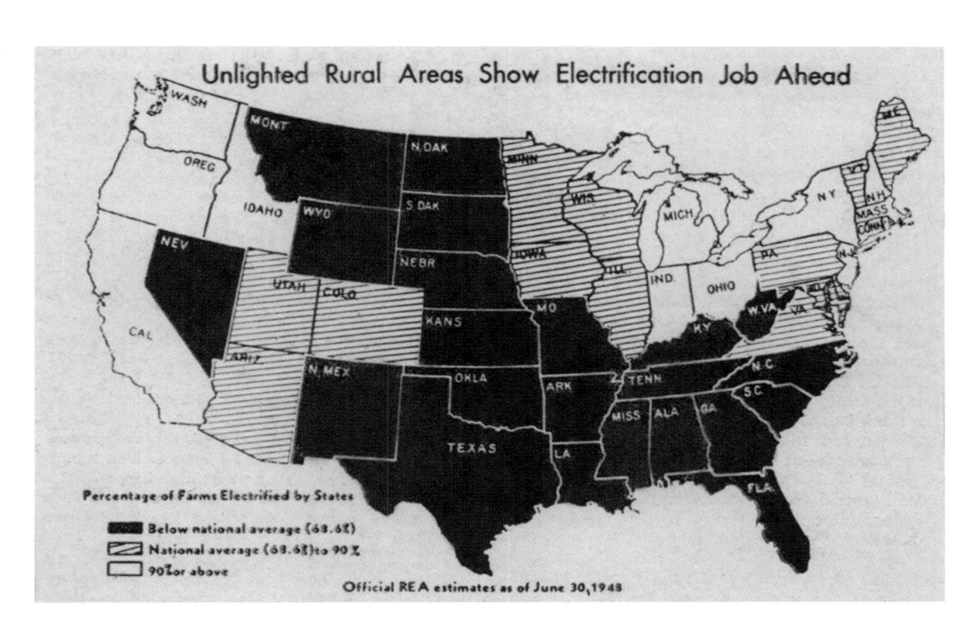

A map of rural electrification in 1948. Fifty percent of Oklahoma farms had been hooked up to electric service as compared to 3 percent when the rural electrification program began just thirteen years earlier.

The Oklahoma Rural News *"Homemaker's Page" featured recipes, household hints, sewing patterns, and tips on saving energy around the home.*

In an April 1983 article from the *Oklahoma Rural News* about the days before electricity, Leo Lawrence recalled the hardships of farm life in rural Oklahoma. "Farmers' wives worked as hard as their husbands. They chopped wood to feed a cast-iron stove, carried water by hand and mended clothing on a treadle sewing machine."

In addition to ease of preparation, the genesis of electricity on the farm meant access to a more robust variety of foods. The electric freezer revolutionized foods available to rural Oklahomans. Previously, fresh meats would only be available during the winter months for fear of spoilage during hot summer days. In the freezer, meats and produce could be stored for use year-round.

In the post-World War II era, all-electric kitchens became more popular in the Oklahoma countryside. The December 1953 edition of the *Oklahoma Rural News* featured a photo of Mrs. Nancy Bishop's electric kitchen, which included an oven, waffle iron, refrigerator, and electric mixer. With the advent of electricity, luxuries began to find their way into the daily diet. "Because we have electricity, we can have ice cream any day," Bishop said.

In an age of post-war affluence, recipes such as Vinegar Cobbler (see page 180), made as a substitute for apple cobbler during the Depression and Dust Bowl days, became a reminder of past hardships. An era of cooking for enjoyment—rather than survival—had begun.

Electricity Revolutionizes Cooking

Once responsible for culling, killing, and deboning under-producing hens, the 1950s homemaker made use of every part of the bird. Nothing was wasted. Today, the majority of chicken recipes call for boneless, skinless chicken breasts. The electrification of Oklahoma farms,

A wood stove used for cooking prior to electricity.

Mrs. Cupp worked to clean out her freezer to prepare to put down chickens and strawberries. The electric freezer allowed families to enjoy meats and nutritious produce year-round.

The 1950s homemaker could be the proud owner of a Kelvinator Electric Range for $239.95.

and the resulting increase in the standard of living, is evident in recipes collected over the years.

The source of ingredients has also changed with time. The majority of today's chicken is not fresh from the farm. And while many people maintain a garden, most produce today is purchased. Canning—once an essential means of food preservation—is now more of a hobby than a necessity. Commercially canned vegetables, soups, and other pre-prepared products are widely used and cake mixes have all but replaced scratch-baked versions.

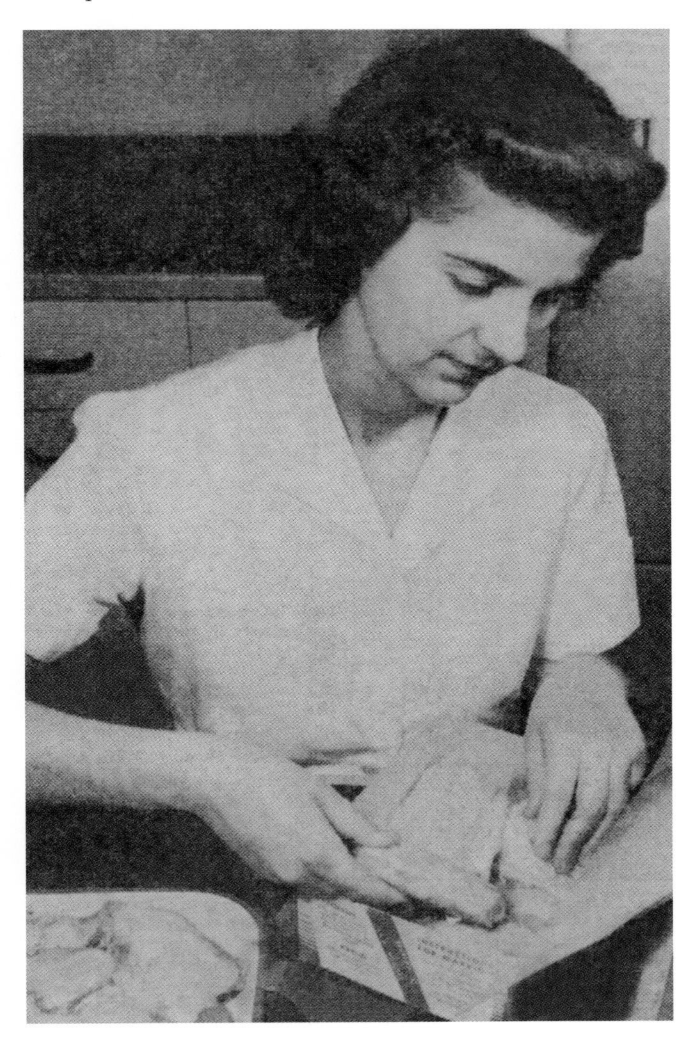

One of the homemaker's duties was preparing whole chickens for the freezer. All parts of the chicken were utilized.

In the 1970s and '80s, such convenience foods became more widely used, as did the microwave ovens utilized to prepare quick meals and TV dinners. A recipe for Beef-Stuffed Tomatoes (see page 116), cooked completely in the microwave, is evidence of this. With most women no longer full-time homemakers, the time available for cooking has been reduced. In many households, food preparation is a shared duty and fast food has become a weeknight staple rather than a special treat.

The Heart of the Home

Just as the kitchen is the heart of the home, the recipes have been an integral element of *Oklahoma Living* magazine from its inception. Will Rogers once said, "We only have one or two wars in a lifetime but we have three meals a day. There is nothing in the world that we do as much of as we do eating."

This cookbook has been compiled to celebrate sixty-five years of this daily ritual of preparing food for Oklahoma families. The recipes have been submitted by faithful readers as well as collected from the magazine's archives. Throughout the cookbook, excerpts from past editions of the *Oklahoma Rural News/Oklahoma Living* magazine have been included to highlight the correlation between electric development and the evolution of cooking. Also spotlighted are recipes that are "Uniquely Oklahoman"—typical Okie fare. If one reads carefully, he or she will find that the recipes themselves tell the story of Oklahoma's history—from the pre-electricity days and into the decades following.

Breakfast & Brunch

Yogurt-Berry Parfait *(see page 25).*

Linda's Breakfast Casserole

"Linemen love it!"

A Cimarron Electric Cooperative lineman wires a pole. Photo courtesy of Cimarron Electric Cooperative.

16-ounce package sausage
12 eggs
4-ounce can diced green chilies
¼ cup sour cream
salt and black pepper
¼ cup half-and-half
1 tube crescent rolls
26-ounce package frozen shredded hash browns
16-ounce package mixed shredded cheese

Preheat the oven to 350°F. Brown and drain the sausage. In a large bowl, whisk together the eggs, chilies, sour cream, salt, pepper, and half-and-half. Grease the bottom and sides of a 9-inch-square baking pan. Spread the crescent rolls in the bottom of the pan and up the sides and press thin. Spread the hash browns over the crescent rolls. Crumble the sausage over the hash browns. Pour the egg mixture over the top and sprinkle with the cheese. Cover the pan with foil and bake for 35 to 40 minutes. Uncover and bake until the middle is fluffy and set. Serve with salsa.

Linda Warner
Cherokee, Okla.
Alfalfa Electric Cooperative

Panhandle Casserole

1 pound lean, hot sausage
1 pound cheddar cheese, shredded
1 ¼ pounds Monterey jack cheese, shredded
3 4-ounce cans green chilies, drained
9 eggs, beaten
1 cup milk
2 tablespoons all-purpose flour
paprika

Preheat the oven to 350°F. Brown and drain the sausage. Layer the sausage, the cheeses, and the chilies in a 9-by-13-inch baking dish. In a medium bowl, combine the eggs, milk, and flour. Pour the egg mixture over the top. Sprinkle with paprika and bake for 40 to 45 minutes.

Sydney Rogers
Enid, Okla.

WE'RE EATING BETTER, THANKS TO FARMER

The people of our country are confronted with high prices, unbelievable interest rates and there's a recession on, but, as a nation, we still eat better for less than we did in 1950. Our prosperity at the table is due to consumer income rising faster than food prices and, in part, is attributable to increased efficiency of the American farmer. Some of the farmer's efficiency is due directly to the rural electric cooperatives (RECs). The electricity made available to farmers by the RECs helps them to grow more food and fiber for our daily needs.

How well is the American consumer doing? Recently released information by the U.S. Department of Agriculture (USDA) compares what the average U.S. factory worker could buy with an hour's pay in 1950 to a similar purchase in 1980. We don't work nearly as long to buy food as we did 30 years ago.

For example, an hour at work in 1950 would buy just over 10 pounds of white bread. But the same hour of work two years ago was good for more than 14 pounds of bread. That same hour of work put three gallons of milk on the table in 1980 as compared to two gallons in 1950. And when it comes to chicken, an hour of labor three decades ago made it possible to buy 2 ½ pounds of frying chicken as compared to four times as much "finger licking" during the more recent comparison period. A worker could buy 8.7 dozen eggs on an hour's pay two years ago, up considerably from the 2.4 dozen he could buy for an hour's work in the opening days of the Korean War.

Much of this abundance of food comes from the increased output of today's farm.

Oklahoma Rural News
August 1982

Breakfast Lasagna

Breakfast Lasagna

1 pound sausage
1 tube crescent rolls
2 cups shredded hash browns
5 eggs
½ cup milk
2 cups shredded cheese

Preheat the oven to 350°F. Brown and drain the sausage. Spread out the crescent rolls in the bottom of a 9-by-13-inch baking dish. Layer the hash browns on top of the crescent rolls. Layer on the sausage. In a medium bowl, whisk together the eggs and milk. Pour the mixture over the sausage. Sprinkle the cheese on top. Bake for 25 to 30 minutes.

Mary Ann Cunningham
Grove, Okla.
Northeast Oklahoma Electric Cooperative

A "**Helpful Hint**" from the February 1953 *Oklahoma Rural News*: When poaching eggs, add a teaspoonful of vinegar to the water in which the eggs are to be cooked. This helps to keep the white from spreading.

Working Man's Quiche

For the crust:
2 cups sifted all-purpose flour
¾ tablespoon salt
⅔ cup cold, unsalted butter
4 to 6 tablespoons ice water

For the filling:
2 red bell peppers
½ pound mushrooms, sliced
1 pound hot sausage
1 bunch green onions, sliced
1 pound Monterey jack cheese, shredded
2 cups heavy cream
3 eggs
2 teaspoons dried parsley
salt and black pepper, to taste

With a fork or pastry cutter, mix the flour, salt, and butter in a medium bowl until the mixture resembles coarse cornmeal. With clean hands, work in 1 tablespoon of ice water at a time until a slightly dry dough ball forms (be careful not to overwork the dough). Wrap the dough ball in plastic wrap and refrigerate for at least 30 minutes. Once it has chilled, roll out the crust and place it in a springform pan or a deep, fluted tart pan with a removable bottom. Refrigerate the rolled shell for at least 1 hour. While the shell is chilling, roast, peel, and chop the bell peppers. Sauté the mushrooms in olive oil. Brown and drain the sausage. Mix the mushrooms, peppers, sausage, green onions, and cheese in a large bowl. In a small bowl, whisk together the cream and eggs. Pour the egg mixture into the large bowl; add the parsley, salt, and pepper and mix to combine. Pour the mixture into the chilled shell and bake for 1 hour at 350°F or until the filling has set. Let the quiche cool on a rack and serve warm.

April 2013
Oklahoma Living

Working Man's Quiche

Corned Beef Hash

1 pound unpeeled red potatoes
2 cups chopped corned beef
2 tablespoons olive oil
1 small onion
4 green onions, chopped

Boil 1 pound of red potatoes until tender. Dice the potatoes into ½-inch chunks. Chop the corned beef into ¼-inch pieces. To a large skillet, add the olive oil and onions. Cook over medium-high heat for approximately 3 minutes to caramelize the onions. Reduce the heat to medium and add the potatoes, corned beef, and green onions. Cook the hash, stirring frequently, until it is heated through.

March 2011
Oklahoma Living

Corned Beef Hash

Mini Egg Casseroles

2 slices sandwich bread
¾ cup cooked sausage crumbles
¾ cup shredded cheddar cheese
8 eggs
⅔ cup milk
1 teaspoon dried thyme
½ teaspoon black pepper

Preheat the oven to 350°F. Grease a muffin pan with cooking spray and set it aside. Cut the bread into ¼-inch cubes. Divide the cubes evenly among the muffin pan's twelve cups. Add 1 tablespoon of sausage and 1 tablespoon of shredded cheese to each cup. In a medium bowl, whisk together the eggs, milk, thyme, and pepper. Fill each muffin cup with the egg mixture. Bake for 15 minutes.

May 2012
Oklahoma Living

A "**Helpful Hint**" from the February 1953 *Oklahoma Rural News*: To reheat coffee cakes and rolls, place them on a baking sheet uncovered, loosely wrap in tin foil or place in a large paper bag, and heat in a 400-degree oven for about 10 minutes.

Melissa's Bacon-Ranch Crescents

1 tube crescent rolls
1 tablespoon ranch dressing
2 tablespoons real bacon bits
½ cup shredded cheese

Preheat the oven to 350°F. Spray a baking sheet with cooking spray. Roll the crescent rolls out into two 4-inch-wide rectangles. Spread ranch onto each section and sprinkle with bacon bits. Top with the cheese. Roll up each rectangle, starting with one of the short sides. Cut each roll into five sections and place them on the baking sheet. Bake for 15 minutes or until crescent rolls are done.

Louise Brandenburg
Fairfax, Okla.
Indian Electric Cooperative

Guam Coffee Cake

2 ½ cups bread flour
¾ cup granulated sugar
1 cup brown sugar
1 teaspoon ground nutmeg
1 teaspoon baking powder
½ teaspoon salt
¾ cup oil
½ cup chopped nuts
½ teaspoon ground cinnamon
1 egg
1 cup buttermilk
1 teaspoon baking soda

Preheat the oven to 375°F. In a medium bowl, combine the flour, sugars, nutmeg, baking powder, and salt. Add the oil and mix well. Remove ¾ cup of the mixture and transfer it to a small bowl. To the small bowl, add the nuts and cinnamon. Set the mixture aside. To the medium bowl, add the egg, buttermilk, and baking soda. Pour the batter into a greased and floured bundt pan. Sprinkle the nut mixture over the top of the batter. Bake for 10 minutes; reduce the oven temperature to 350°F and continue baking for 20 to 25 minutes or until a toothpick inserted in the center comes out clean.

Anne Thurston
Tulsa, Okla.

Cream Cheese Coffee Cake

For the cake:
2 cups all-purpose flour
1 teaspoon baking powder
½ teaspoon baking soda
¼ teaspoon salt
½ cup room-temperature butter or margarine
8 ounces room-temperature cream cheese
1 ¼ cups granulated sugar
2 extra-large eggs
1 teaspoon vanilla extract
¼ cup milk

For the topping:
⅓ cup brown sugar
⅓ cup all-purpose flour
½ teaspoon ground cinnamon
2 tablespoons butter

For the glaze (optional):
powdered sugar
half-and-half or cream

Preheat the oven to 350°F. In a medium bowl, combine the flour, baking powder, baking soda, and salt. In a separate bowl, combine the butter and cream cheese with an electric mixer. Add the sugar, eggs, vanilla, and milk. Mix in the dry ingredients. Pour the batter into a greased and floured 9-by-13-inch baking pan. In a medium bowl, combine the topping ingredients and sprinkle over the top of the batter. Bake for 30 minutes. If desired, make a glaze by combining powdered sugar and half-and-half or cream and drizzle over the cooled cake.

Judith Whelchel
Blanchard, Okla.
Oklahoma Electric Cooperative

Dehl Twins' Monkey Bread

1 cup granulated sugar
1 tablespoon ground cinnamon
1 cup butter
1 package frozen roll dough, thawed

Combine the sugar and cinnamon in a small bowl. Melt the butter in a separate bowl. Pinch off golf ball-size pieces of dough; dip them into the butter and roll them in the sugar mixture. Place dough balls in an angel food cake pan. Let rise in a warm place until they double in size. Bake according to frozen roll package directions.

Jeanette Duncan
Howe, Okla.
Kiamichi Electric Cooperative

Uniquely Oklahoman

Prairie Pancakes

- 6 tablespoons vegetable oil
- 1 egg
- 1 ¼ cups milk
- 1 ¼ cups all-purpose flour
- ¼ cup wheat germ
- ½ cup granulated sugar
- 1 tablespoon baking powder
- ¼ teaspoon salt

Grease and preheat a griddle. In a large bowl, whisk together the oil, egg, and milk. In a medium bowl, combine the dry ingredients. Add the flour mixture to the large bowl and mix well. Cook on a hot griddle.

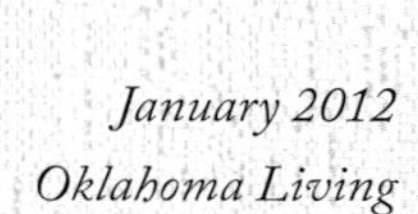

January 2012
Oklahoma Living

Multi-Grain Waffles

- 2 cups buttermilk
- ½ cup old-fashioned rolled oats
- ⅔ cup whole-wheat flour
- ⅔ cup all-purpose flour
- ¼ cup toasted wheat germ or cornmeal
- 1 ½ teaspoons baking powder
- ½ teaspoon baking soda
- ¼ teaspoon salt
- 1 teaspoon ground cinnamon
- 2 eggs, beaten
- ¼ cup packed brown sugar
- 1 tablespoon canola oil
- 2 teaspoons vanilla extract
- ¼ cup chopped pecans (optional)

In a medium bowl, mix the buttermilk and oats; let stand for 15 minutes. Combine the flours, wheat germ, baking powder, baking soda, salt, and cinnamon in a large bowl. Stir the eggs, sugar, oil, and vanilla into the oat mixture. Add the wet ingredients to the dry ingredients and mix until just moistened. Coat a waffle iron with cooking spray and preheat. Cover three-fourths of the waffle iron surface with batter and cook until the waffle is golden brown, about 4 to 5 minutes. The batter can also be cooked as pancakes.

Lisa Richard
Hollis, Okla.
Harmon Electric Association

A "**Helpful Hint**" from the February 1953 *Oklahoma Rural News*: Baking soda may be used to remove grease and discoloration from a waffle iron.

Overnight Belgian Waffles

½ cup lukewarm water (105°F)
1 tablespoon granulated sugar
1 package active dry yeast
2 cups whole milk, warmed (105°F)
½ cup unsalted butter, melted and cooled
1 teaspoon salt
2 cups all-purpose flour
2 eggs, beaten
2 teaspoons vanilla extract
¼ teaspoon baking soda

Combine the water, sugar, and yeast. Let stand until foamy, about 10 minutes. Stir in the milk, butter, and salt. Beat in the flour until smooth using an electric mixer on low speed. Wrap the bowl tightly with plastic wrap and let it stand overnight (at least 8 hours) on the countertop. Do not refrigerate. Preheat the waffle iron. While the waffle iron is heating, stir the eggs, vanilla, and baking soda into the batter. Pour the batter into the waffle iron and cook until crisp.

Lin Archer
Harrah, Okla.
Oklahoma Electric Cooperative

Gingerbread Waffles and Whipped Cream

"For something new in the ever-popular waffle department, surprise the breakfasters with these delicious gingerbread waffles."

2 cups sifted all-purpose flour
¾ teaspoon baking powder
½ teaspoon salt
1 tablespoon granulated sugar
1 teaspoon ground ginger
1 teaspoon ground cinnamon
2 eggs, separated
1 cup molasses
½ cup sour milk or buttermilk
⅓ cup shortening, melted

Sift together the dry ingredients. Combine well-beaten yolks with molasses. Add the molasses mixture to the dry ingredients alternately with the sour milk or buttermilk, beating until smooth. Add the melted shortening and fold in stiffly beaten egg whites. Pour about ¼ cup of batter onto a hot waffle iron. Cook for 3 to 5 minutes. Serve hot with whipped cream.

January 1948
Oklahoma Rural News

Baked French Toast

For the French toast:

1 baguette
1 ½ cups milk
1 ½ cups heavy cream
3 eggs
1 teaspoon vanilla extract
⅛ teaspoon salt
2 tablespoons granulated sugar
1 teaspoon ground cinnamon
⅛ teaspoon ground mace (optional)
⅛ teaspoon ground cardamom (optional)

For the topping:

½ teaspoon ground cinnamon
1 tablespoon granulated sugar

Cut the baguette diagonally into twelve ¾-inch-thick slices. Allow the bread to dry out overnight. The next morning, preheat the oven to 425°F, with a rack positioned in the middle of the oven. Arrange the baguette slices in a greased 9-by-13-inch baking dish. In a medium bowl, whisk together the remaining ingredients. Pour the liquid mixture over the baguette slices and let stand for 5 minutes. After 5 minutes, flip the slices. Continue to flip the slices at 5-minute intervals for a total of 30 minutes. Most of the liquid should be absorbed. If not, pour off excess, leaving no more than a ½-inch of liquid in the bottom of the dish. For the topping, mix the cinnamon and sugar in a small bowl. Sprinkle evenly over the top of the baguette slices. Bake for 30 to 35 minutes or until the tops are puffed up and golden brown. Serve with maple syrup or honey.

Rachael Wattanasak
Tulsa, Okla.

Baked French Toast

A "**Helpful Hint**" from the February 1953 *Oklahoma Rural News*: To sour milk or cream, add 1 tablespoon of vinegar or lemon juice to 1 cup sweet milk or cream.

Hardeman Guest House Caramel French Toast

- 1 ½ cups packed dark brown sugar
- ¾ cup unsalted butter
- ¼ cup plus 1 tablespoon dark corn syrup
- 1 loaf French bread, cut into 1 ½-inch slices
- 5 eggs, beaten
- 2 cups milk
- 1 tablespoon vanilla extract
- ¼ teaspoon salt
- 3 tablespoons granulated sugar
- 1 ½ teaspoons ground cinnamon
- ¼ cup butter, melted

Combine the brown sugar, butter, and corn syrup in a small saucepan. Cook over medium heat, stirring constantly for 5 minutes or until the mixture is bubbly. Pour into a lightly greased 9-by-13-inch baking dish. Arrange bread slices over the syrup mixture. In a medium bowl, combine the eggs, milk, vanilla, and salt; stir well. Pour over the bread slices. Cover and chill for at least 8 hours. When ready to bake, combine the granulated sugar and cinnamon and sprinkle evenly over the soaked bread. Drizzle with melted butter. Bake, uncovered, at 350°F for 45 to 50 minutes or until golden brown and bubbly. Serve immediately.

Sherri Snider
Tulsa, Okla.

Sour Milk Doughnuts

- 1 egg, beaten
- 1 cup granulated sugar, plus extra for coating the doughnuts
- 1 cup sour milk
- 1 ½ tablespoons lard, melted
- 4 cups all-purpose flour
- 1 ½ teaspoons baking soda
- 2 teaspoons cream of tartar
- 1 ½ teaspoons salt
- 1 teaspoon ground nutmeg
- oil for frying

Combine the egg, sugar, milk, and lard in a large bowl. In a separate bowl, sift the flour with the remaining dry ingredients. Combine with the wet ingredients. Shape and fry the doughnuts in deep fat. Turn the doughnuts as soon as they come to the top of the fat and frequently afterwards. Drain on paper. Transfer to a paper bag filled with sugar and shake to coat.

July 1949
Oklahoma Rural News

A "**Helpful Hint**" from the June 1960 *Oklahoma Rural News*: When frying doughnuts, you can prevent them from absorbing too much fat if you add a spoonful of vinegar to the hot fat when cooking.

Easy Donut Holes

Easy Donut Holes

vegetable oil for frying
1 tube refrigerated buttermilk biscuit dough
½ cup granulated sugar
1 ½ teaspoons ground cinnamon
½ cup powdered sugar
2 brown paper lunch bags

Pour the vegetable oil into a medium saucepan. Heat the oil to 350°F. While the oil is preheating, open the biscuit dough and use a 1-inch round cutter to cut circles from the dough. Add the granulated sugar and cinnamon to one of the brown paper bags. Fold the top over to close the bag and shake it to mix the cinnamon with the sugar. Add the powdered sugar to the other bag. Fry the dough circles in the preheated oil and cook until golden. Remove the donuts with a slotted spoon and place them into one of the sugar-filled paper bags. Shake the bag to coat.

May 2012
Oklahoma Living

Yogurt-Berry Parfait

3 strawberries, hulled
¼ cup fresh blueberries
¼ cup fresh raspberries
½ cup vanilla Greek yogurt
¼ cup granola

Cut the strawberries into bite-size pieces. Mix with the blueberries and raspberries. Spoon a few tablespoons of the mixed berries into the bottom of a clear glass. Top with a layer of granola and a layer of yogurt. Continue layering fruit with granola and yogurt until the glass is filled. Finish with a layer of yogurt, a sprinkle of granola, and berries to garnish.

May 2012
Oklahoma Living

Uniquely Oklahoman

Sand Plum Jelly

4 pounds fresh sand plums
5 cups granulated sugar
1 package pectin, such as Sure-Jell

In large pot, cover the sand plums with water. Bring to a boil and cook until tender. Run plums and liquids through a colander, reserving the juice. Strain the juice through cheesecloth and discard the solids. Measure 4 cups of the juice and put it back into the large pot. Mix the pectin with the juice. Cook over medium heat. When the mixture comes to a rolling boil, add the sugar and boil for 4 minutes. Let cool for a few minutes, then skim the bubbles off the surface with a metal spoon. Pour hot jelly into hot, sterile jars. Clean off the tops of the jars with a damp cloth. Put lids on the jars and screw on rings. Let cool and listen for the "pop" when the jars seal.

S. Francie Russell
Meeker, Okla.
Canadian Valley Electric Cooperative

Tangy Lemon Curd

3 medium eggs, beaten
2 cups granulated sugar
¾ cup lemon juice
2 teaspoons lemon zest
¾ cup butter, cubed
2 drops lemon oil (not extract)

In a large, heavy saucepan over medium heat, whisk together the eggs, sugar, lemon juice, and lemon zest until blended. Add the butter and lemon oil. Cook, stirring constantly, until the mixture is thickened and coats the back of a metal spoon. Transfer to a bowl and let cool for 10 minutes. Cover and place in the refrigerator until chilled. Great with waffles, bread, or ice cream.

Trisha Smith
Gage, Okla.

Citrus Marmalade

Citrus Marmalade

1 grapefruit
1 orange
1 lemon
3 ½ quarts cold water
5 pounds granulated sugar
1 teaspoon salt

Cut the fruit into thin slices, discarding the seeds. Place the fruit in a pot and cover with the cold water. Let stand overnight. The next day, cook the fruit until it is tender, about 45 to 60 minutes. Let stand overnight. On the third day, add the sugar and the salt and cook on high, stirring occasionally, until it reaches 220°F (the jellying point) on a candy thermometer. Remove any foam from the jelly and pour the jelly into sterilized jars. Process for 5 minutes in a boiling water bath.

Dave Law
Ringling, Okla.

Corn Cob Jelly

Corn cob jelly traditionally uses red field corn cobs; yellow cobs will also work but the resulting jelly will be yellow in color.

12 red corn cobs
water
2 tablespoons lemon juice
1 package pectin, such as Sure-Jell
3 cups granulated sugar

Break the cobs into pieces and boil for 30 minutes. Strain the liquid and discard the cobs. Add additional water to make 3 cups of liquid, if needed. Add the lemon juice and pectin and bring the liquid to a rolling boil. Add the sugar and boil 2 to 3 minutes more until it reaches the jelly stage. The finished product tastes a lot like apple jelly and has an attractive reddish color.

April 1964
Oklahoma Rural News

Uniquely Oklahoman

Chocolate Gravy

2 tablespoons butter or margarine
1 heaping tablespoon cocoa powder
¼ cup granulated sugar
dash salt
1 tablespoon all-purpose flour or cornstarch
2 cups milk

In a skillet or medium saucepan, melt the butter or margarine over medium-low heat. Add the cocoa powder, sugar, and salt. Stir until the sugar has dissolved. Add the flour or cornstarch and the milk, stirring constantly until combined. Cook over medium-low heat until bubbly and thickened, stirring occasionally. Let the gravy simmer a few minutes at a time without stirring. If the gravy is too thick, add more milk and stir.

Sherry Crowson Canfield
Del City, Okla.

Breads, Biscuits, & Muffins

Cranberry-Orange Bread (see page 30).

Carrot Bread

¾ cup vegetable oil
2 eggs, beaten
1 cup granulated sugar
1 teaspoon baking soda
¼ teaspoon salt
1 teaspoon ground cinnamon
1 teaspoon vanilla extract
1 cup finely grated raw carrot
½ cup chopped nuts or flaked coconut

Preheat the oven to 325°F. In a medium bowl, cream together the oil, eggs, and sugar. Sift the dry ingredients and stir them into the oil mixture, along with the vanilla. Add carrots and nuts and mix well. Bake in a greased and floured loaf pan for 1 ½ hours.

May 1975
Oklahoma Rural News

Uniquely Oklahoman

Lydia Wade's Cornbread

"This is my grandmother's recipe. She came to Kenefic, Okla., with her parents, brothers, and sisters during Indian Territory days. She would sometimes grind the corn grown in her garden for cornbread. Her granddaughters and great-granddaughters still make cornbread using this recipe today."

1 to 3 tablespoons vegetable oil or meat drippings
1 cup yellow cornmeal
½ cup all-purpose flour
2 teaspoons baking powder
1 teaspoon salt
1 to 3 tablespoons granulated sugar
1 cup milk
1 egg

Preheat the oven to 450°F. Add 1 tablespoon of oil or meat drippings to an 8-inch iron skillet and place the skillet inside the oven while it is preheating. In a medium bowl, sift together the dry ingredients. Add the milk, egg, and remaining oil or meat drippings and mix well. When the batter is ready, remove the skillet from the oven and place it on top of the stove on a hot burner. Pour the batter into the hot pan. Bake for 25 minutes or until golden brown.

Lydia L. Roper
Caddo, Okla.
Southeastern Electric Cooperative

Uniquely Oklahoman

Bean Bread

1 cup cornmeal
½ cup all-purpose flour
2 teaspoons baking powder
1 tablespoon granulated sugar
2 cups milk
¼ cup shortening, melted
1 beaten egg
2 tablespoons honey
4 cups brown beans, drained

Preheat the oven to 450°F. In a medium bowl, mix all of the ingredients, except the beans, thoroughly. Fold in the beans. Pour the batter into a greased, preheated pan. Bake for 30 minutes or until brown.

The Cherokee Nation

Cranberry-Orange Bread with Cranberry-Orange Butter

For the bread:
2 cups all-purpose flour
1 cup granulated sugar
1½ teaspoons baking powder
½ teaspoon baking soda
1 teaspoon salt
¾ cup orange juice
1 tablespoon orange zest
1 egg, beaten
3 tablespoons sour cream
4 tablespoons butter, melted
½ cup chopped nuts (optional)
2 cups chopped cranberries

For the butter:
½ cup butter, melted
2 tablespoons orange marmalade
2 tablespoons whole cranberry sauce

Preheat the oven to 350°F. Sift together the flour, sugar, baking powder, baking soda, and salt. Combine the orange juice and zest with the egg; pour into the dry ingredients, mixing enough to just dampen. Add the sour cream and butter; mix. Fold in the nuts and cranberries. Spoon the batter into a greased 9-by-5-inch loaf pan. Spread the corners and sides slightly higher than the center. Bake for 1 hour or until the crust is golden brown and a toothpick inserted in the center comes out clean. Remove from the pan. Store overnight for easy slicing. To make the butter, beat the butter until fluffy and mix in the marmalade and cranberry sauce.

Reta Bowen
Asher, Okla.
Canadian Valley Electric Cooperative

Cheesy Pear Nut Bread

1 ¾ cups all-purpose flour
¾ cup whole-wheat flour
1 cup packed brown sugar
3 ½ teaspoons baking powder
1 tablespoon lemon zest
½ teaspoon salt
1 ¼ cups milk
¼ cup butter, melted
1 egg
1 teaspoon vanilla extract
1 ½ cups shredded cheddar cheese
1 cup chopped, peeled baking pears
½ cup chopped pecans

Preheat the oven to 350°F. Combine the flours, sugar, baking powder, lemon zest, and salt in large bowl. Add the milk, butter, egg, and vanilla. Stir until dry ingredients are just moistened. Stir in the cheese, pears, and pecans. Spoon the mixture into a buttered loaf pan. Bake for 55 to 60 minutes or until a toothpick inserted in the center comes out clean. Cool in the pan on a cooling rack for 15 minutes. Remove from the pan, cool completely on the cooling rack, and wrap in plastic wrap. Let stand for 24 hours at room temperature before slicing.

October 1985
Oklahoma Rural News

Cheesy Pear Nut Bread

Zucchini Bread

3 eggs, beaten
1 cup oil
2 cups granulated sugar
2 cups grated, unpeeled zucchini
1 teaspoon vanilla extract
3 cups all-purpose flour
1 teaspoon salt
½ teaspoon baking powder
1 teaspoon baking soda
¾ teaspoon ground cinnamon
1 cup chopped nuts

Preheat the oven to 350°F. In a medium bowl, combine the eggs, oil, sugar, zucchini, and vanilla. Sift the dry ingredients together and add them to the egg mixture. Grease the bottoms of two large loaf pans or three to four smaller ones. Fit waxed paper over the grease. Fill the pans and bake for 1 hour or until a toothpick inserted in the center comes out clean. Cut around the edges with a sharp knife and turn out onto a cooling rack. Peel off the waxed paper and turn the loaves upright on the rack. Let cool. Bread can be frozen if not served on the first or second day. Keep tightly wrapped to prevent it from drying out.

Donna Franklin
Ada, Okla.
People's Electric Cooperative

Citrus Nut Bread

2 cups all-purpose flour
¾ cup granulated sugar
½ teaspoon salt
½ teaspoon baking soda
½ cup chopped pecans or walnuts
1 tablespoon orange zest
¼ teaspoon lemon zest
1 egg
¾ cup orange juice
2 tablespoons lemon juice
2 tablespoons vegetable oil
1 teaspoon orange extract

Preheat the oven to 350°F. In a large bowl, combine the flour, sugar, salt, and baking soda. Stir in the nuts and orange and lemon zests. In a medium bowl, combine the remaining ingredients. Mix the wet ingredients into the dry ingredients, stirring until just moistened. Spoon the batter into a greased and floured loaf pan. Bake for 50 to 60 minutes or until a toothpick inserted in the center comes out clean. Cool the bread in the pan for in 10 minutes; remove the bread and cool on a cooling rack.

Ronald Smith
Tulsa, Okla.
Verdigris Valley Electric Cooperative

Orange Bread

For the bread:

3 cups all-purpose flour
1 ½ teaspoons baking powder
1 ⅛ cups sunflower or canola oil
1 teaspoon orange zest
1 ½ teaspoons almond flavoring
1 ½ teaspoons butter flavoring
½ teaspoon vanilla extract
1 ½ teaspoons salt
3 eggs
1 ½ cups milk
2 ¼ cups granulated sugar
1 ½ tablespoons poppy seeds

For the glaze:

½ teaspoon almond flavoring
½ teaspoon butter flavoring
¼ cup orange juice concentrate
¾ cup granulated sugar

Preheat the oven to 350°F. For the bread, beat all ingredients together in a large bowl. Pour the batter into two greased and floured loaf pans. Bake for 1 hour. While the bread is baking, mix the glaze ingredients together in a small bowl. When the bread is done, use a toothpick to poke multiple holes in the loaves. Pour the glaze over the bread.

Bonnie Jobe
Tahlequah, Okla.
Lake Region Electric Cooperative

Grandpa Veith's Oatmeal Bread

2 cups boiling water
2 cups oats
1 tablespoon butter, margarine, or oil
2 teaspoons salt
½ cup sorghum
½ cup lukewarm water
1 ½ tablespoons yeast
½ tablespoon granulated sugar
5 to 6 cups all-purpose flour

In a medium bowl, combine the boiling water, oats, butter, and salt. Let cool until lukewarm. In another bowl, mix the sorghum, water, yeast, and sugar. Add the cooled oatmeal mixture. Stir in 5 to 6 cups of flour. Place the dough in a greased bowl. Cover and allow it to rise until it doubles in size. Punch down the dough and form it into two loaves. Place the dough into two greased loaf pans. Let them rise again until they double in size. Bake at 350°F for 30 minutes or more. Remove the loaves from the pans and butter the tops.

Mary J. Moerbe
Blackwell, Okla.
Kay Electric Cooperative

Hoe Bread

"This recipe gets its name from the old-time farm homemaker who could hoe in the garden until thirty minutes before mealtime and then have a delicious hot bread for dinner."

¾ cup shortening
2 cups all-purpose flour
2 tablespoons plus 1 teaspoon baking powder
1 teaspoon salt
2 tablespoons granulated sugar
1 ¼ cups milk
3 eggs

Preheat the oven to 450°F. Melt the shortening in a 12-inch iron skillet. Transfer to a small bowl. In a large bowl, sift together the flour, baking powder, salt, and sugar. Add the milk, eggs, and ½ cup of the melted shortening, stirring well after each addition. Pour the batter into the iron skillet; spoon the remaining ¼ cup of shortening over the batter. Bake for 10 minutes. Reduce the heat to 400°F and bake for 10 more minutes.

Latrecha Easley Hall
Coweta, Okla.
Lake Region Electric Cooperative

Uniquely Oklahoman

Fried Indian Bread

2 packages active dry yeast
1 ½ cups warm water
1 cup milk
2 teaspoons salt
2 ½ cups granulated sugar
2 tablespoons shortening
2 eggs
6 ½ to 7 cups all-purpose flour
oil for frying
powdered sugar

In a large bowl, dissolve the yeast in the warm water. Add the milk, salt, sugar, shortening, and eggs and mix well. Stir in the flour, 1 cup at a time. When the dough becomes too thick to stir, knead in the remaining flour by hand. Cover the dough and allow it to rise for 1 hour. Cut the dough in half and roll each half out with a rolling pin, not too thinly. Cut the dough into triangles, cover them, and allow them to rise until they double in size. Fry the triangles until golden in oil heated to 375°F. Place the powdered sugar in a paper bag and shake the cooked bread in it to coat.

August 1995
Oklahoma Living

No-Knead Whole-Wheat Bread

1 ½ cups whole-wheat flour
1 tablespoon salt
2 packages active dry yeast
1 cup water
1 cup milk
¼ cup honey
¼ cup oil
1 egg
2 ½ to 3 cups all-purpose flour

Combine the whole-wheat flour, salt, and yeast in a large bowl. In a medium saucepan, heat the water, milk, honey, and oil over low heat until very warm (120 to 130°F). Add the liquids and the egg to the flour mixture. Blend with an electric mixer on low speed until moistened; increase speed to medium and beat for 3 more minutes. Stir in the white flour by the spoonful to form stiff dough. Cover the dough and let it rise in a warm place until it doubles in size, about 50 minutes. Place the dough into a greased 9-by-5-inch loaf pan or two 8-by-4-inch loaf pans. Bake at 375°F for 45 to 50 minutes for the single loaf or 30 to 35 minutes for the two loaves. Remove the bread from the pan immediately and cool on a cooling rack. Brush the top or tops with butter.

March 1980
Oklahoma Rural News

Challah Bread

4 ¾ cups all-purpose flour
1 tablespoon powdered milk
2 tablespoons granulated sugar
1 teaspoon salt
½ teaspoon instant yeast
3 eggs
3 tablespoons oil
1 ⅓ cup plus 2 tablespoons water

In a large bowl or stand mixer bowl, combine the dry ingredients using an electric mixer with a dough hook. Add 2 eggs and 2 tablespoons of oil and mix on medium speed. Add 1 ⅓ cups of water, a little bit at a time, until the dough forms a ball. Continue mixing until the dough pulls away from the sides of the bowl and produces a distinctive "slapping" noise. Cover the bowl and allow the dough to rest for 15 to 20 minutes. Divide the dough into three equal parts. Roll each piece out into a 12-inch-long rope. Pinch the tops together and braid. Secure the dough tightly at the bottom of the braid. Place the braid on a parchment-lined baking sheet. Cover; let rise until it doubles in size. In a small bowl, whisk together the remaining egg and the remaining 2 tablespoons of water. Brush the egg wash over the dough. Bake the bread at 350°F for 30 minutes or until golden brown. Remove from the oven; brush with the remaining tablespoon of oil and cool on a cooling rack.

July 1991
Oklahoma Rural News

Beer Bread

3 cups self-rising flour
1 tablespoon granulated sugar
12 ounces beer

Preheat the oven to 375°F. In a medium bowl, combine all ingredients. Transfer the batter to a greased loaf pan. Bake for 45 minutes.

Patricia Babcock
Kingston, Okla.
Red River Valley Rural Electric Association

Oklahoma Cheese Toast

4 slices white bread
4 slices American cheese
granulated sugar

Arrange the bread on a baking sheet. Place a slice of cheese on each piece of bread. Broil until the cheese melts and the bread toasts. Watch carefully so it does not burn. Sprinkle the hot bread with sugar.

Glory King
Oklahoma City, Okla.

Cheesy Garlic-Dill Toast

½ cup butter
½ cup mayonnaise
½ teaspoon garlic salt or garlic powder
1 teaspoon dill
1 cup Monterey jack cheese
1 cup cheddar cheese
1 loaf French bread

Preheat the oven to 350°F. Soften the butter, but do not melt. Combine the butter with the mayonnaise, garlic salt or powder, dill, and cheeses. Slice the French bread and spread each piece with a thin layer of the butter mixture. Place the slices on a baking sheet and bake until the bottom of the bread is lightly crisp.

Mary Louise Dolezal
Perry, Okla.
Central Rural Electric Cooperative

Spoon Hot Rolls

- 1 package active dry yeast
- 1 cup warm water
- 2 tablespoons granulated sugar
- 3 tablespoons butter or margarine, melted
- 1 egg, beaten
- 2 ¼ cups all-purpose flour

In a large bowl, dissolve the yeast in the water. Add the remaining ingredients, mix well, and cover. Allow the dough to rise until doubled. Spoon the dough into greased muffin tins. Allow the rolls to rise for 30 more minutes. Bake at 425°F for 15 minutes.

November 1994
Oklahoma Living

Uniquely Oklahoman

Persimmon Date Nut Bread

- ¼ cup plus 2 tablespoons softened butter or margarine
- 1 cup granulated sugar
- 2 eggs
- 1 teaspoon baking soda
- 1 cup persimmon pulp
- 2 cups all-purpose flour
- 1 teaspoon baking powder
- ½ teaspoon salt
- ½ teaspoon ground cinnamon
- ½ teaspoon ground nutmeg
- ½ teaspoon ground cloves
- 1 cup chopped pecans
- 1 cup chopped dates

Preheat the oven to 350°F. In a medium bowl, cream the butter and sugar together. Add the eggs one at a time, beating well after each addition. In a small bowl, combine the baking soda and persimmon pulp until the soda is dissolved. Add to the butter mixture, blending well. In another medium bowl, combine the flour, baking powder, salt, cinnamon, nutmeg, and cloves. Gradually add the dry ingredients to the wet ingredients, mixing well. Stir in the pecans and dates. Pour the batter into a greased 9-by-5-inch loaf pan. Bake for 80 minutes or until a toothpick inserted in the center comes out clean. Cool in the pan for 10 minutes; remove from the pan and cool on a cooling rack.

December 1982
Oklahoma Rural News

Fly-Off-the-Plate Hot Rolls

"My mother would have turned up her nose at bread made with all water. She would have sniffed and called it 'water bread' as if that were the worst kind of bread to make. You could use water instead of the milk in this recipe, a half stick of butter, and no egg and still have tasty hot rolls."

2 packages active dry yeast
½ cup warm water
scant ½ cup granulated sugar
1 teaspoon salt
2 cups milk
½ cup butter
1 egg
6 cups all-purpose flour

In a large bowl, combine the yeast, water, sugar, and salt. Let the mixture stand for a few minutes. Warm the milk and butter in the microwave until the butter melts. The mixture should not be too hot to touch. If it is, let it cool. Break the egg into the milk mixture and stir until smooth. Pour the milk mixture into the yeast and stir in 5 cups of the flour. Turn the dough out onto a floured surface. Knead in an additional cup of flour, or a little more, until the dough is not sticky and forms a ball. Grease the bowl and place the dough into the bowl; turn the dough so the greased side is facing up. Cover the bowl and let the dough rise until it almost doubles in size. Gently push the dough down and form the dough into egg-size balls. Place them into a greased 11-by-15-inch baking pan. Cover and let rise until they nearly double in size. Bake at 375°F for 25 to 28 minutes until browned; check the rolls after 20 minutes. Serve hot.

Lin Archer
Harrah, Okla.
Oklahoma Electric Cooperative

A homemaker looks on with anticipation as an electric range is delivered to her newly electrified home. Photo courtesy of Cimarron Electric Cooperative.

Uniquely Oklahoman

Land Run Sweet Biscuits

- 2 cups all-purpose flour
- 1 tablespoon baking powder
- ½ teaspoon salt
- 1 cup sweet cream butter
- 1 tablespoon molasses
- ⅔ cup buttermilk
- 1 cup syrup
- 1 cup chopped pecans

Preheat the oven to 450°F. Add dry ingredients to a large bowl and mix by hand. Using two knives or a large fork, work in the butter and molasses until the mixture is crumbly. Make a well in the middle of the flour mixture and add the buttermilk. Mix with a large fork until dough begins to stick together, then knead into a soft ball with floured hands to prevent sticking. Pinch dough into fifteen 1 ½-inch balls and flatten to ½-inch-thick circles. Place the biscuits (not touching) into two warm, greased cast-iron skillets. Bake for 8 to 10 minutes. When biscuits are lightly browned on top, remove from the oven and pour syrup over all the biscuits in the skillet, then sprinkle the chopped pecans on top. Place the skillets back in the oven under the broiler for about a minute to caramelize the syrup and pecans. Serve warm.

June 2007
Oklahoma Living

Crispy Whole-Wheat Drop Biscuits

- 1 cup whole-wheat flour
- 1 ½ cups all-purpose flour
- ½ teaspoon salt
- 1 tablespoon baking powder
- ½ cup canola oil
- 1 cup reduced-fat milk

Preheat the oven to 450°F. In a medium bowl, whisk together the dry ingredients. Make a well in the middle and add the oil and milk. Mix until combined. Drop by rounded tablespoons onto a greased baking sheet. Flatten them a little or leave them in mounds. Bake for 20 to 25 minutes or until golden brown and crispy.

Jeanette Duncan
Howe, Okla.
Kiamichi Electric Cooperative

7-Up Biscuits

½ cup sour cream
2 cups baking mix, such as Bisquick
½ cup lemon-lime soda, such as 7-Up
¼ cup butter, melted

Preheat the oven to 450°F. Cut the sour cream into the baking mix. Add the lemon-lime soda. Sprinkle the counter with baking mix, place the dough on top, and pat the dough out. Pour the butter into a 9-inch-square pan. Cut out biscuits with a biscuit cutter and arrange them on top of the butter. Bake for 12 to 15 minutes or until golden brown.

Laura Sandness
Prague, Okla.
Canadian Valley Electric Cooperative

Sweet Potato Biscuits

The Stewart family, dairy farmers, used 300 pounds of ice each day to cool milk before electricity came to their farm. Mrs. Stewart was able to churn butter with an electric mixer in her updated kitchen.

2 cups all-purpose flour
⅔ cup granulated sugar
1½ teaspoons salt
2 tablespoons baking powder
¼ cup shortening
2 cups mashed sweet potatoes
¼ cup milk

Preheat the oven to 475°F. In a medium bowl, sift together the flour, sugar, salt, and baking powder. Cut in the shortening until the mixture resembles cornmeal. Stir in the sweet potatoes and gradually add the milk to form a soft dough. Turn the dough out onto a lightly floured surface and knead it lightly. Roll or pat the dough into ½-inch thickness and cut biscuits out with a biscuit cutter. Place biscuits onto a greased baking sheet and bake for 12 to 15 minutes.

August 1995
Oklahoma Living

Uniquely Oklahoman

Dutch Oven Sourdough Biscuits

3 cups sourdough starter
1 package active dry yeast
⅓ cup oil
2 teaspoons salt
2 ½ tablespoons baking powder
5 ½ tablespoons granulated sugar
2 ½ to 3 cups all-purpose flour

In a medium bowl, combine the sourdough starter and yeast. Mix well; allow the mixture to stand for a few minutes. Add the oil, salt, baking powder, and sugar. Mix well with a whisk. Gradually add the flour until the dough reaches the desired texture. Knead the dough and roll out onto a floured surface to ½-inch thickness. Cut out biscuits with a biscuit cutter. Place biscuits in a buttered 16-inch Dutch oven or pan. Allow the biscuits to rise and cook with coals on top and bottom for about 15 to 20 minutes or until golden brown.

Sourdough Starter
4 cups warm water
1 package dry yeast
5 tablespoons granulated sugar
4 cups all-purpose flour
1 potato, peeled and quartered

Pour the warm water into a large bowl. Stir in the yeast and allow the mixture to stand for a few minutes. Whisk in the sugar and gradually blend in the flour. Place the potato in the bottom of a crock jar, along with the starter. Cover with a towel and stir occasionally. Starter will be ready in 12 hours.

Recharging Starter
After 3 cups of the starter is used, replace with:
1 ½ cups warm water
2 tablespoons granulated sugar
1 ½ cups all-purpose flour

April 2001
Oklahoma Living

Honey Poppy Seed Biscuits

½ cup creamed cottage cheese
¼ cup milk
2 tablespoons honey
2 ¼ cups packaged biscuit mix
1 tablespoon poppy seeds

In a medium bowl, combine the cottage cheese, milk, and honey; blend until almost smooth. Prepare the biscuit mix according to package directions, substituting the cottage cheese mixture for the liquid, and add poppy seeds. Add another 1 or 2 tablespoons of milk if necessary. Bake as directed on the biscuit mix package.

Helen Stangl
Perry, Okla.
Central Rural Electric Cooperative

Sausage Ball Muffins

2 cups baking mix, such as Bisquick
1 pound pork sausage
3 cups shredded sharp cheddar cheese
¼ cup finely chopped onion
1 tablespoon garlic powder
¼ teaspoon hot sauce

Preheat the oven to 400°F. Mix all of the ingredients in a large bowl, pressing together by hand. Spoon rounded tablespoons into greased mini-muffin pans. Bake for 13 to 16 minutes. Serve warm.

Frances H. Gardner
Bartlesville, Okla.
Verdigris Valley Electric Cooperative

Sour Cream Scones

1 cup sour cream
1 teaspoon baking soda
4 cups all-purpose flour
1 cup granulated sugar
2 teaspoons baking powder
¼ teaspoon cream of tartar
1 teaspoon salt
1 cup butter
1 egg
1 cup raisins (optional)

Preheat the oven to 350°F. Lightly grease a large baking sheet. In a small bowl, blend the sour cream and baking soda; set aside. In a large bowl, mix the flour, sugar, baking powder, cream of tartar, and salt. Cut in the butter. Stir the sour cream mixture and egg into the flour mixture until just moistened. Mix in the raisins. Turn the dough out onto a lightly floured surface and knead briefly. Roll or pat the dough into a ¾-inch-thick round. Cut into twelve wedges and place them two inches apart on the prepared baking sheet. Bake for 12 to 15 minutes, until golden brown on the bottom.

Mary J. Moerbe
Blackwell, Okla.
Kay Electric Cooperative

Cherry Scones

Cherry Scones

2 cups all-purpose flour
1 tablespoon granulated sugar
1 teaspoon baking powder
½ teaspoon baking soda
¼ teaspoon salt
¾ cup butter
⅔ cup dried cherries
2 eggs, beaten
⅔ cup buttermilk

Preheat the oven to 375°F. Combine the flour, sugar, baking powder, baking soda, and salt in a bowl. Cut the butter into the dry ingredients with a pastry blender. Stir in the cherries. Combine the eggs and buttermilk and stir into the flour mixture until a dough forms. Turn the dough out onto a lightly floured surface and knead it lightly. Pat it into a 10-inch circle. Cut the circle into twelve wedges. Or, instead of cutting wedges from the dough, spoon golf ball-size pieces of the dough onto a baking sheet. Bake for 16 to 19 minutes or until golden brown.

Joanne Smith
Collinsville, Okla.
Verdigris Valley Electric Cooperative

Cheese Muffins

Cheese Muffins

"There will be calls for 'seconds' as the butter melts on these hot Cheese Muffins. Let this bread accompany a fresh fruit plate or a tossed green salad."

2 cups sifted all-purpose flour
1 tablespoon baking powder
½ teaspoon salt
1 cup shredded American cheese
1 egg, beaten
1 cup milk
2 tablespoons melted shortening

Preheat the oven to 425°F. Sift together the flour, baking powder, and salt in a medium bowl. Add the cheese and mix lightly. Add the liquids to the flour mixture, stirring until flour is just moistened. Fill greased muffin cups two-thirds full. Bake for 20 minutes.

April 1953
Oklahoma Rural News

Bran Muffins

"This is a muffin mix that I would make when my daughter was small. She was not much of a breakfast eater but she loved these. She is thirty-four now and she still makes them for her family."

15-ounce box raisin bran cereal
3 cups granulated sugar
5 cups all-purpose flour
2 teaspoons salt
2 teaspoons ground cinnamon
4 eggs, beaten
1 quart buttermilk
1 cup oil

Preheat the oven to 375°F. Combine the dry ingredients in a large bowl. Blend in the remaining ingredients. Bake in a greased muffin pan for 20 minutes.

Elena Backus
Ada, Okla.

Bran Muffins

Appetizers

Cowboy Caviar (see page 48).

Fresh Orange Salsa

½ cup diced fresh orange segments
1 cup diced Roma tomato
1 tablespoon finely chopped red onion
1 teaspoon minced jalapeño
2 tablespoons chopped cilantro
⅛ teaspoon salt

Combine all ingredients in a medium bowl and toss gently to mix. Cover and refrigerate until serving. Great with tortilla chips or on fish or chicken.

Kathy Henderson
Lake Hudson, Okla.
Northeast Oklahoma Electric Cooperative

Fresh Orange Salsa

Oklahoma Caviar

2 cans black-eyed peas, drained
2 cups Italian dressing
1 cup chopped green onion
1 cup chopped red onion
2 cups chopped green bell pepper
½ cup chopped jalapeño pepper
1 small jar pimientos
1 tablespoon chopped garlic

Combine all ingredients in a large bowl. Cover and refrigerate for 24 hours. Serve with tortilla chips.

Mary Ann Cunningham
Grove, Okla.
Northeast Oklahoma Electric Cooperative

Uniquely Oklahoman

Cowboy Caviar

15-ounce can shoepeg corn
15-ounce can black-eyed peas
1 avocado, peeled and diced
⅔ cup chopped cilantro
2 green onions, chopped
4 ripe tomatoes, diced
2 cloves garlic, crushed
¼ cup olive oil
¼ cup red wine vinegar
¾ teaspoon salt
⅛ teaspoon black pepper
1 tablespoon ground cumin

Drain the corn and black-eyed peas. Combine the corn, black-eyed peas, avocado, cilantro, green onions, and tomatoes in medium bowl. Mix well. In a small bowl, combine the garlic, olive oil, vinegar, salt, pepper, and cumin. Whisk until well blended. Pour the mixture over the vegetables and toss to coat. Serve with tortilla chips.

S. Francie Russell
Meeker, Okla.
Canadian Valley Electric Cooperative

Tangy Meatballs

For the meatballs:
2 eggs
2 cups quick-cooking oats
12-ounce can evaporated milk
1 cup chopped onion
1 teaspoon salt
½ teaspoon black pepper
½ teaspoon garlic powder
3 pounds lean ground beef

For the sauce:
2 cups ketchup
1 ½ cups packed brown sugar
½ cup chopped onion
2 teaspoons liquid smoke
½ teaspoon garlic powder

Preheat the oven to 375°F. In large bowl, beat the eggs; add the oats, milk, onion, salt, pepper, and garlic powder. Add the ground beef, mixing well. Shape into 1 ½-inch balls. Place into two 9-by-13-inch baking dishes and bake for 30 minutes. Remove from the oven and drain. In a saucepan, bring combined sauce ingredients to boil. Pour over meatballs. Return to the oven and bake, uncovered, for 20 minutes.

Becky Sparks
Blair, Okla.
Southwest Rural Electric Association

Nana Lou's Meatballs

For the meatballs:
1 pound lean ground beef
1 cup cooked rice
salt and black pepper
2 eggs
1 teaspoon Worcestershire sauce
1 cup saltine cracker crumbs
1 onion, chopped

For the sauce:
1 cup cream of mushroom soup
1 cup milk
1 tablespoon seasoning sauce, such as Kitchen Bouquet

Preheat the oven to 350°F. To make the meatballs, mix all ingredients well and form into balls. Place in a covered baking dish. Mix the sauce ingredients in a medium bowl and pour over the meatballs. Bake for 45 to 60 minutes.

Betty Branch
Wynnewood, Okla.

Sweet and Spicy Meatballs

3 cups picante sauce
½ cup grape jelly
2 pounds fully cooked frozen meatballs

Place the picante sauce and jelly in a slow cooker and mix well. Add the frozen meatballs. Cook for 4 hours on low, stirring occasionally to coat the meatballs with the sauce. Meatballs taste even better the second day.

November 2012
Oklahoma Living

Bourbon Franks

14 ounces ketchup
1 cup bourbon
1 cup brown sugar
2 pounds hot dogs, such as Hebrew Nationals, cut into chunks

In a large saucepan, mix the ketchup, bourbon, and brown sugar. Cover and simmer for a couple of hours, stirring occasionally. Transfer to a covered container and refrigerate overnight. Reheat the sauce until hot, add hot dog chunks, and simmer until heated through.

Judith Whelchel
Blanchard, Okla.
Oklahoma Electric Cooperative

Ham and Cheese Ball

1 large package sliced ham
2 8-ounce packages cream cheese
3 tablespoons flavor-enhancer seasoning, such as Accent
6 green onions, chopped

Set aside 4 slices of ham; chop remaining ham into small pieces. Mix together with the remaining ingredients; shape into a ball. Wrap in reserved sliced ham. Chill for at least 2 hours. Serve with crackers.

JoAnn Parker
Western Farmers Electric Cooperative

Chocolate Chip Cheese Ball

Chocolate Chip Cheese Ball

8 ounces cream cheese, softened
½ cup softened butter
¼ teaspoon vanilla extract
¾ cup powdered sugar
2 tablespoons brown sugar
¾ cup mini semisweet chocolate chips
¾ cup finely chopped toasted pecans

In a large bowl, beat the cream cheese, butter, and vanilla until fluffy. Gradually add the sugars; beat until just combined. Stir in the chocolate chips. Cover and refrigerate for 2 hours. Place the cream cheese mixture on a large piece of plastic wrap; shape into a ball. Refrigerate for at least 1 hour. Just before serving, roll the cheese ball in pecans. Serve with graham crackers, animal crackers, vanilla wafers, or ginger snaps.

Lydia L. Roper
Caddo, Okla.
Southeastern Electric Cooperative

Onion Soufflé

24 ounces cream cheese, softened
1 ½ cups chopped onion
½ cup mayonnaise
1 cup grated Parmesan cheese

Preheat the oven to 350°F. In a large bowl, combine all ingredients and mix well. Transfer to a 9-by-13-inch baking dish sprayed with cooking spray. Bake for 20 to 25 minutes or until lightly browned on top. Serve hot with pita chips or crackers.

Loveta Hammond
Oklahoma City, Okla.
East Central Oklahoma Electric Cooperative

TOTAL ELECTRIC LIVING IS ECONOMICAL

If you have heard the old story that total electric living costs too much, let's look into the Jack Kay home located two miles north of Wilburton in the Centerpoint community. The total cost of electricity for the 1,500-square-foot home of Mr. and Mrs. Jack Kay averaged only $20.38 per month during the 12 months of 1966.

There is no gas going into the home. Electricity furnishes power for water heating, an automatic washer, dryer, freezer, the usual small appliances, lighting, heating the entire house, and pumping the water for this family of four. In fact, all the expense that is normally classed as utility bills, except the telephone, is paid in one account to Kiamichi Electric Cooperative with headquarters in Wilburton.

Mrs. Kay has cooked electrically for many years and told us, "When I used to hear ads about the advantages of electric cooking I didn't believe it because I had nothing to compare it with. However, when we first moved to Wilburton we rented an apartment that had a gas range. Now I believe it. The electric range is much faster and so much cleaner—there is no comparison."

Most people are slow to change from what they have been used to for years but the change to electric heating across the state is nothing short of phenomenal as people began to learn the many advantages of electric living. Mrs. Kay told us she has sold some of her neighbors because of the advantages they have experienced.

With the advantages of safety, economy and cleanliness, just to mention a few, it is hard to imagine why everyone doesn't make the switch to living better electrically.

Oklahoma Rural News
March 1967

Layered BLT Dip

- 8 ounces cream cheese
- ½ cup mayonnaise
- ¼ cup shredded cheese, plus additional for topping
- shredded lettuce
- 1 package real bacon bits
- 4 Roma tomatoes, chopped

Combine the cream cheese, mayonnaise, and ¼ cup of the shredded cheese. Spread in the bottom of a serving dish. Layer the remaining ingredients on top. Top with additional shredded cheese. Chill and serve.

Pat Sewell
Porum, Okla.

Buffalo Chicken Dip

Buffalo Chicken Dip

- 1 package ranch dressing mix
- ¾ cup hot sauce, such as Frank's
- 16 ounces cream cheese, softened
- 2 cups shredded rotisserie chicken
- 2 cups shredded cheddar cheese

Preheat the oven to 350°F. Spray a baking dish with cooking spray. In a medium bowl, combine the ranch dressing mix, hot sauce, and cream cheese. Add the chicken and 1 cup of the cheese. Transfer the mixture to the baking dish. Top with the remaining cup of cheese. Bake for 30 minutes.

Tory Tedder
Norman, Okla.
Oklahoma Electric Cooperative

Ray B's Dip

8 ounces sour cream
2 packages ranch dressing mix
16 ounces cream cheese
2 cups buttermilk
2 cups mayonnaise
1 cup chopped pecans
1 teaspoon garlic salt
¼ teaspoon black pepper
1 lemon, juiced

In a large bowl, combine all ingredients; mix well. Refrigerate.

Shirley Weaver
Grandfield, Okla.

White Queso

1 pound sausage
2 10-ounce cans diced tomatoes and green chilies, such as Rotel
16 ounces cream cheese
16 ounces sour cream

Brown and drain the sausage. Place with the remaining ingredients in a slow cooker. Heat for 30 to 45 minutes, stirring occasionally. Serve with tortilla chips.

Sandra Hook
Norman, Okla.
Oklahoma Electric Cooperative

Zesty Italian Veggie Dip

16 ounces cream cheese, softened
1 package dry Italian dressing mix, such as Good Seasons
2 tablespoons vegetable juice, such as V-8

In a large bowl, blend the cream cheese, Italian dressing mix, and vegetable juice. Adjust the amount of vegetable juice so that the mixture is a dip consistency. Chill for at least 2 hours. Serve with raw veggies.

Susan Akers
Harrah, Okla.
Central Rural Electric Cooperative

Jalapeño Popper Spread

16 ounces cream cheese
1 cup mayonnaise
4-ounce can chopped green chilies
4-ounce can chopped jalapeños
1 cup finely shredded cheese

In a medium bowl, combine the cream cheese and mayonnaise. Stir in the chilies and jalapeños. Transfer the mixture to a microwave-safe dish. Top with the shredded cheese. Heat for 3 minutes. Serve with tortilla chips.

Mrs. Charles Kerfoot
Perry, Okla.
Canadian Valley and Kay Electric Cooperatives

Spicy Spinach Dip

Spicy Spinach Dip

16 ounces frozen spinach
¼ cup finely chopped red onion
10-ounce can diced tomatoes and green chilies, such as Rotel
2 8-ounce packages cream cheese
¼ cup grated Parmesan cheese
1 cup shredded Colby jack cheese

Defrost the spinach and press to drain excess water. Place with the remaining ingredients, except the Colby jack cheese, in a microwave-safe bowl. Heat, stirring every minute, for approximately 5 minutes or until the ingredients are well combined. Add the Colby jack cheese and heat for another minute. Serve hot with tortilla chips.

February 2012
Oklahoma Living

Pineapple Spread

1 small can crushed pineapple, drained
2 8-ounce packages room-temperature cream cheese
1 medium onion, finely chopped

In a medium bowl, combine the pineapple and cream cheese. Mix well. Stir in the chopped onion. Serve with butter crackers.

Annavee Kirby-Denny
Colcord, Okla.
Northeast Oklahoma Electric Cooperative

Deviled Egg Balls

8 hard-boiled eggs
3 strips bacon
¼ cup mayonnaise
1 teaspoon minced onion
½ teaspoon salt
½ teaspoon black pepper
¼ teaspoon mustard
1 cup shredded cheddar cheese

Chop the eggs into small pieces. Cook, drain, and crumble the bacon. In a medium bowl, combine the eggs, bacon, mayonnaise, onion, salt, pepper, and mustard. Mix well. Form the mixture into 1-inch balls. Roll each ball in shredded cheese. Refrigerate until serving.

Novell Wilson
Tulsa, Okla.
Verdigris Valley Electric Cooperative

Turkey Cranberry Braid

2 cups chopped, cooked turkey
1 cup shredded Swiss cheese
¼ cup Parmesan cheese
¼ cup finely chopped onion
⅓ cup dried cranberries
3 tablespoons chopped Italian parsley
½ cup mayonnaise
1 tablespoon Dijon mustard
¼ teaspoon black pepper
2 tubes refrigerated crescent roll dough
1 egg white

Preheat the oven to 375°F. In a large bowl, mix together the turkey, cheeses, onion, cranberries, parsley, mayonnaise, mustard, and pepper. Unroll the crescent rolls and arrange them in a rectangle on a large sheet of parchment paper. Use a rolling pin to roll the seams together. Spread the turkey filling down the center of the rectangle, leaving approximately three inches on each side. Use a knife or pizza cutter to cut strips—1 ½ inches wide and 3 inches long—into the sides along the length of the rectangle. Pick up one of the strips, twist it once, and lay it on top of the filling. Continue with all of the strips, alternating sides. Whisk the egg white and brush it over the braided dough. Transfer the parchment to a baking sheet. Bake for 25 to 30 minutes until the pastry is golden.

November 2012
Oklahoma Living

Tortilla Roll-ups

Tortilla Roll-ups

8 ounces cream cheese, softened
¼ cup picante sauce
8 large tortillas
¾ pound thinly sliced turkey pastrami

In a small bowl, mix the cream cheese and picante sauce until smooth. Spread the mixture on the tortillas. Place 3 or 4 pieces of turkey pastrami on each tortilla. Roll the tortillas tightly and wrap in plastic wrap. Chill overnight. Slice into small pieces.

Rachel Meredith
Sallisaw, Okla.
Cookson Hills Electric Cooperative

Tomato-Basil Elephant Ears

- 1 ¼ cups chopped sun-dried tomatoes
- 3 tablespoons chopped garlic
- 5 cups packed basil leaves
- 1 teaspoon salt
- 1 teaspoon black pepper
- ¾ cup olive oil
- 1 cup grated Parmesan cheese
- 1 sheet puff pastry
- 1 egg
- 1 tablespoon water

Preheat the oven to 400°F. Place the sun-dried tomatoes and garlic in a food processor. Process for 30 seconds. Add the basil, salt, and pepper. With the processor running, slowly pour the oil into the bowl and process until pureed. Add the Parmesan cheese and puree for 15 seconds. Set aside. Unfold the puff pastry and place it on a lightly floured surface. Gently roll the dough into a 13-inch square. Spread the paste over the top of the pastry. Fold the sides of the square toward the center so they go halfway to the middle. Fold them again so the two folds meet exactly in the middle of the dough. Then fold one half over the other half as though closing a book. You will have six layers. Cut the dough in half, and in half again, continuing until thin slices are formed. Place the slices on a baking sheet lined with parchment paper. In a small bowl, whisk together the egg and the water. Brush each slice with the egg wash. Bake for 6 minutes. Turn each slice over and bake for 5 more minutes.

Sierra D. Jones
Moore, Okla.
Oklahoma Electric Cooperative

Mini Twice-Baked Potatoes

- 24 2-inch-diameter potatoes
- 2 tablespoons olive oil
- salt and black pepper
- ½ cup sour cream
- ¼ cup Parmesan cheese
- ¼ cup finely chopped chives
- ¼ cup real bacon bits

Preheat the oven to 400°F. Place the potatoes on a baking sheet. Drizzle them with olive oil and sprinkle them with salt and pepper. Bake the potatoes for 20 to 25 minutes until they are tender and a fork can be easily inserted in the flesh. Remove them from the oven and allow them to cool. Once they are cool, cut off the top skin of each potato. Carefully scoop out the flesh and transfer it to a medium bowl. Use a fork or potato masher to mash the potato flesh with the sour cream, Parmesan cheese, 3 tablespoons of the chives, the bacon, and salt and pepper to taste. Spoon the mixture back into the potatoes. Potatoes can be made up to this stage and covered well and refrigerated for a day or two. Before serving, preheat the oven to 450°F. Bake for 8 to 10 minutes. Garnish with remaining chives. Serve hot.

November 2012
Oklahoma Living

Baked Brie in Puff Pastry

1 sheet frozen puff pastry, thawed
8-ounce wheel brie
3 tablespoons orange marmalade
2 tablespoons dried cranberries
1 egg white

Preheat the oven to 350°F. Place the puff pastry on a nonstick baking sheet. Cut the brie in half horizontally. Place the bottom half of the brie on the puff pastry. Spread the marmalade over the brie and sprinkle the cranberries over the top. Place the upper half of the brie on top. Pull the puff pastry up over the brie. Seal the pastry around the brie and trim excess dough. Flip the package over so the seam is on the bottom. Whisk the egg white and brush it over the top and sides of the pastry. Bake for 20 to 25 minutes until the pastry is golden. Serve hot with crackers.

November 2012
Oklahoma Living

Baked Brie in Puff Pastry

Bruschetta Two Ways

Bruschetta Two Ways

4 cloves garlic
½ cup olive oil
1 baguette

Several hours or a day before making the bruschetta, slice the garlic and place it in a small bowl with the olive oil so that the garlic flavor will infuse the oil. Preheat the oven to 450°F. Slice the baguette diagonally into ½-inch pieces. Brush both sides of each piece of bread with the garlic-infused oil and place the slices onto a baking sheet. Bake for about 5 minutes, until the bread starts to brown. Serve with one of the toppings below.

Goat Cheese, Pesto, and Pine Nut Bruschetta:
½ cup pine nuts
½ cup fresh basil leaves
1 clove garlic (from the garlic oil)
2 tablespoons olive oil
2 tablespoons grated Parmesan or Romano cheese
4 ounces spreadable goat cheese

In a small skillet over medium heat, toast the pine nuts until they are golden. Shake the skillet often and watch the nuts closely so they do not burn. To make the pesto, place the basil, ¼ cup of the toasted pine nuts, and the garlic in a food processor. Pulse to combine. Once combined, turn the food processor on and slowly add the oil. Then, turn the food processor off and add the Parmesan or Romano cheese. Pulse to combine. To assemble the bruschetta, spread each slice of toasted bread with a layer of goat cheese, a layer of pesto, and top with a few toasted pine nuts.

Tomato, Onion, and Basil Bruschetta:
2 cups cherry tomatoes
¼ cup basil leaves
¼ small red onion
sliced garlic (from the garlic oil)
1 tablespoon olive oil
¼ teaspoon salt
¼ teaspoon black pepper

Halve the cherry tomatoes and place them in a small bowl. Cut or tear the basil leaves into small pieces and add them to the tomatoes. Finely chop the red onion and add it to the bowl. Remove the garlic slices from the garlic-infused oil and mix them in with the tomatoes. Toss the mixture with the olive oil, salt, and pepper. Place it on top of the toasted bread immediately before serving.

August 2011
Oklahoma Living

Soups, Chilis, & Stews

Asian Chicken Noodle Soup (see page 64).

Creamy Broccoli Orzo Soup

3 stalks celery, chopped
1 green or red bell pepper, diced
1 small onion, diced
2 cloves garlic, minced
1 large carrot, grated
1 tablespoon olive oil
1 teaspoon basil
1 teaspoon thyme
1 teaspoon celery seeds
6 cups vegetable broth
3 cups broccoli, very coarsely chopped
1 cup uncooked orzo pasta
2 tablespoons white miso paste
¾ cup raw cashews
1 cup water
½ cup nutritional yeast
salt, to taste

In a large soup pot, sauté the celery, bell pepper, onion, garlic, and carrot in the oil until the onion is translucent. Add the spices and stir well. Add the broth and broccoli to the sautéed mixture. Add pasta, stirring occasionally so it does not stick. Simmer for 20 minutes. In a blender, process the miso paste, cashews, water, and yeast. Add to the soup pot and simmer for 10 minutes. Taste for salt and add water to adjust the consistency to your liking.

Jennifer Dempsey
Oklahoma Association of Electric Cooperatives

Slow Cooker Chicken Noodle Soup

1 can chicken broth
1 can cooked chicken
1 can diced tomatoes
1 package frozen mixed vegetables
1 cup water
½ cup white wine
1 tablespoon poultry seasoning
pinch salt
pinch black pepper
½ package frozen noodles

Combine all ingredients, except the noodles, in a slow cooker. Cook on low for 2 hours. Add the noodles and continue cooking for 2 more hours.

LaDale Hymer
Cleveland, Okla.
Indian Electric Cooperative

Asian Chicken Noodle Soup

1 chicken breast
4 cups low-sodium chicken stock
1 carrot, peeled and thinly sliced
1 cup water
2 tablespoons low-sodium soy sauce
½ teaspoon white pepper
1 tablespoon freshly grated ginger
3 cloves garlic, minced
4 ounces fresh mushrooms, such as shiitake or oyster, sliced
1 cup snow peas
¼ pound rice noodles

To a large pot, add the chicken breast, chicken stock, and carrot. Cover the pot and bring it to a boil. Once it boils, reduce the heat to a simmer and continue to cook until the chicken breast is fully cooked. Remove the chicken breast from the pot. Discard any skin and bones and shred the meat. Return the meat to the pot, along with the water, soy sauce, white pepper, ginger, garlic, and mushrooms. Bring the soup back to a boil, then reduce to a simmer and cook for 10 minutes. Add the snow peas and the rice noodles, cover the pot, and cook until the noodles are tender, about 5 minutes.

January 2013
Oklahoma Living

Jill's Favorite Tortilla Soup

3 tablespoons olive or grapeseed oil, plus additional for frying
7 wheat tortillas
6 cloves garlic, minced
1 tablespoon chopped fresh cilantro or parsley
2 11-ounce cans tomato puree
2 quarts chicken broth
1 teaspoon ground cumin
2 teaspoons chili powder
2 bay leaves
⅛ teaspoon ground red pepper
2 boneless, skinless chicken breasts, cut into strips
1 avocado, peeled and chopped
1 cup shredded mozzarella cheese

In a Dutch oven or heavy soup pot, heat 3 tablespoons of oil over medium heat. Chop 4 of the tortillas and cook them with the garlic and cilantro in the hot oil until the tortillas are soft. Add the tomato puree and chicken broth, cumin, chili power, bay leaves, and red pepper. Bring to a boil, cover, reduce the heat, and simmer for 30 minutes. Remove and discard the bay leaves. While the soup is cooking, cut the remaining 3 tortillas into strips. Pour oil to depth of 1 inch into a large heavy skillet. Fry strips in hot oil over medium heat until browned. Remove tortillas, drain on paper towels, and set aside. Reserve ½ tablespoon of the oil in the skillet, add the chicken strips, and cook for about 10 minutes or until fully cooked. Spoon the soup into bowls; add chicken strips, avocado, and cheese. Top with the fried tortilla strips.

Sue Robinson
Glencoe, Okla.
Central Rural Electric Cooperative

Chicken Fiesta Soup

Chicken Fiesta Soup

- 1 green bell pepper, chopped
- 1 sweet yellow onion, chopped
- 2 cloves garlic, minced
- 4 cups chicken broth
- 1 cup garden salsa
- 1 cup frozen corn, thawed
- 14 ½-ounce can diced tomatoes
- 15-ounce can black beans, drained and rinsed
- 15-ounce can dark red kidney beans, drained and rinsed
- 1 teaspoon ground cumin
- 1 teaspoon chili powder
- 1 teaspoon garlic powder
- 2 boneless, skinless chicken breasts, cooked and diced

Spray a large stockpot with nonstick cooking spray; place over medium-high heat. Sauté bell pepper and onions for 4 to 5 minutes or until softened; add garlic and sauté for 1 minute. Add the remaining ingredients to the pot. Bring the soup to a boil, then reduce the heat and simmer for 15 minutes. Serve with fresh cilantro, diced avocado, shredded cheese, and sour cream.

April 2013
Oklahoma Living

Daddy Jim's Taco Soup

1 medium onion, chopped
2 tablespoons olive oil
2 pounds ground beef
2 4-ounce cans chopped green chilies
1 package ranch dressing mix
2 packages taco seasoning
28-ounce can diced tomatoes, undrained
2 15-ounce cans pinto beans, undrained
15-ounce can black beans, undrained
15-ounce can ranch-style beans, undrained
2 15-ounce cans golden hominy, undrained

In a large pot over medium-low heat, sauté the onion in the olive oil until tender. Transfer to a small bowl and set aside. Brown the ground beef in the skillet; drain. Mix in the onions and green chilies. Add the ranch dressing mix and taco seasoning and stir well. Add the remaining ingredients. Simmer for 20 to 30 minutes. Serve over chips with shredded cheese and sour cream.

Jim Darnell
Apache, Okla.
Cotton Electric Cooperative

Angela's Tamale Soup

32-ounce can beef broth
16-ounce can pinto beans
11-ounce can Mexicorn, drained
15-ounce can yellow hominy, drained
1 can diced tomatoes and green chilies, such as Rotel
1 teaspoon chili powder
1 teaspoon ground cumin
¼ teaspoon garlic powder
salt and black pepper, to taste
28-ounce can beef tamales

Combine all ingredients, except tamales, in a large pot. Cook over low heat until flavors are blended. Remove the tamales from the can, remove the wrappers, and cut into 1-inch pieces. (This process is messy, but worth it.) Add the tamales to the soup and heat thoroughly. Serve with shredded cheese, sour cream, and chopped green onions if desired.

Angela Daugherty
Western Farmers Electric Cooperative

A "**Helpful Hint**" from the February 1953 *Oklahoma Rural News*: To remove excessive salt from soups, drop a sliced raw potato into the soup and boil for five or six minutes, then remove.

Quick and Easy Soup

- 2 pounds ground beef
- 2 cans ranch-style beans
- 2 cans chicken and rice soup
- 16 ounces tomato sauce
- 1 can diced tomatoes and green chilies, such as Rotel

In a large pot, brown the ground beef; drain. Add remaining ingredients and heat through.

Lisa Richard
Hollis, Okla.
Harmon Electric Association

Lentil Soup

- 1 tablespoon olive oil
- 1 tablespoon minced garlic
- ½ cup chopped onion
- 1 stalk celery, finely chopped
- 1 carrot, finely chopped
- 1 teaspoon black pepper
- 1 teaspoon ground cumin
- ½ pound lentils, rinsed
- 4 cups low-sodium chicken broth
- 2 cups water
- 1 link smoked turkey sausage, diced
- 1 bay leaf
- salt, to taste

To a large, heavy-bottomed pot or Dutch oven, add the olive oil, garlic, onion, celery, carrot, pepper, and cumin. Cook over low heat for 5 minutes. Add the lentils, broth, water, sausage, and bay leaf. Cover the pot and bring to a boil. Reduce the heat to low and simmer for 20 to 25 minutes or until the lentils are tender but not mushy. Add additional salt to taste and additional liquid if desired.

January 2013
Oklahoma Living

Lentil Soup

Curried Pumpkin Soup

2 tablespoons olive oil
2 carrots, peeled and chopped
1 small onion, chopped
1 stalk celery, chopped
1 apple, peeled, cored, and chopped
3 cloves garlic, minced
1 small potato
1 quart chicken broth
29 ounces pumpkin puree
½ cup heavy cream
1 tablespoon yellow curry powder
salt and black pepper

Add the olive oil to a large pot along with the carrot, onion, celery, apple, and garlic. Cook over low heat, stirring occasionally, until the vegetables and apple are soft, about 15 minutes. Meanwhile, peel and chop the potato. Once the vegetables are cooked, add the chicken stock, pumpkin puree, and potato to the pot. Cover and cook for about 15 minutes, until the potato is soft. Gradually transfer the soup to a food processor or blender and puree after each addition. Return the soup to the pot and add the heavy cream, curry powder, and salt and pepper to taste. This produces a thick soup. For a thinner soup, omit the potato.

November 2011
Oklahoma Living

Curried Pumpkin Soup

Uniquely Oklahoman

Red Dirt Chili

- 3 pounds roast
- 2 tablespoons vegetable oil
- 1 large onion, chopped
- 32-ounce can tomatoes
- 24-ounce can tomato sauce
- 4 to 6 cloves garlic, minced
- 1 tablespoon ground cumin
- 2 teaspoons paprika
- 2 tablespoons chili powder
- 1 tablespoon cayenne pepper
- 1 tablespoon cocoa powder
- 12 ounces beer
- 1 tablespoon granulated sugar

Trim the fat from the roast and cut it into small cubes. To a large, heavy cooking pot over medium heat, add the oil, meat, and onions. Brown the meat and cook the onions until they are transparent. Add the tomatoes and tomato sauce, breaking or chopping the tomatoes as needed. Add the remaining ingredients. Cook uncovered over low heat for 4 hours or until meat is tender, stirring often. If the chili becomes too thick, add additional beer or water.

January 2012
Oklahoma Living

White Christmas Chili

- 8 boneless, skinless chicken breasts
- 2 medium onions, chopped
- 2 cloves garlic, minced
- 1 tablespoon olive or grapeseed oil
- 2 14 ½-ounce cans chicken broth
- 4 15-ounce cans cannellini beans, drained and rinsed
- 15-ounce can cannellini beans, drained, rinsed, and mashed
- 2 4 ½-ounce cans chopped green chilies
- 1 teaspoon salt
- ¾ teaspoon dried oregano
- 1 teaspoon ground cumin
- ½ teaspoon chili powder
- ½ teaspoon black pepper
- ⅛ teaspoon ground red pepper
- ⅛ teaspoon ground cloves

Cut chicken into bite-size pieces. In a Dutch oven or heavy soup pot over medium heat, sauté the chicken, onions, and garlic in the oil for about 10 minutes or until chicken is done. Stir in the broth, beans, chilies, salt, oregano, cumin, chili powder, black and red pepper, and cloves. Bring to a boil, cover, reduce the heat, and simmer for 30 minutes. Serve with fresh chopped cilantro.

Sue Robinson
Glencoe, Okla.
Central Rural Electric Cooperative

Josh's Chili

- 1 pound ground beef
- 1 pound sausage, such as Blue and Gold
- ½ packet chili seasoning, such as Williams
- 1 can mushrooms
- 1 bar chocolate, such as Hershey's
- ½ cup brown sugar
- 1 large can mild chili beans, such as Bush's
- 1 medium can tomato sauce
- 1 medium can diced tomatoes

Brown the ground beef and sausage. Add chili seasoning and mix. Drain the grease and combine the meat with the remaining ingredients. Simmer.

Diane Ferrell
Cherokee, Okla.
Alfalfa Electric Cooperative

Pumpkin, White Bean, and Sausage Stew

2 tablespoons olive oil
4 pork or turkey Italian sausage links
1 small onion, chopped
2 carrots, peeled and sliced into 1-inch pieces
2 small potatoes, cut into 1-inch pieces
1 small pumpkin, peeled, seeded, and cut into 1-inch pieces
1 teaspoon ground cumin
1 cup white beans, drained
2 tablespoons chopped parsley
4 cups chicken broth
1 bay leaf
salt and black pepper, to taste

In heavy 6-quart pot, heat the olive oil over medium-high heat. Brown the sausage links on all sides for about 10 minutes, then transfer to a plate. Add the onion to the pot and cook until translucent, about 5 minutes. Add the remaining ingredients and bring to a boil. Return the sausage to the pot and reduce the heat to medium-low. Cook for about 30 minutes, until the pumpkin is tender when pierced with a fork. Adjust the seasonings with salt and pepper to taste. Remove bay leaf before serving.

Jennifer Dempsey
Oklahoma Association of Electric Cooperatives

Slow Cooker Beef and Potato Stew

1 teaspoon salt
1 teaspoon black pepper
1 teaspoon garlic powder
1 teaspoon flour
1 pound beef stew meat
1 can tomato soup
1 can diced tomatoes
½ cup white wine
1 tablespoon soy sauce
1 cup beef broth
1 cup corn
1 cup carrots, sliced
1 sweet potato, chopped
1 onion, diced
1 bell pepper, diced
1 teaspoon paprika

Sift together salt, pepper, garlic powder, and flour and combine with beef in a zip-top bag; shake to coat the meat. Add all of the ingredients to a slow cooker and cook on low for 8 hours.

LaDale Hymer
Cleveland, Okla.
Indian Electric Cooperative

Triple Bean Chowder

- ½ cup chopped onion
- ½ cup chopped celery
- ¼ cup butter
- 2 teaspoons flour
- 6 tablespoons Worcestershire sauce
- ¾ teaspoon salt
- ¼ teaspoon black pepper
- ⅔ teaspoon paprika
- 4 cups milk
- 1 can condensed chicken broth
- 1 can garbanzo beans, drained and rinsed
- 1 can red kidney beans, drained and rinsed
- 9-ounce package frozen cut green beans, cooked and drained

Sauté the onion and celery in butter in a large saucepan over low heat until tender, about 5 minutes. Stir in the flour, Worcestershire sauce, salt, pepper, and paprika until smooth. Remove from heat and gradually stir in the milk and chicken broth. Heat to boiling, stirring constantly; boil and stir for 1 minute. Add the beans and simmer uncovered for 5 minutes, stirring occasionally.

January 1984
Oklahoma Rural News

Triple Bean Chowder

Chicken-Corn Chowder

1 1/2 pounds chicken wings, tips removed
1 1/2 cups chicken broth
2 teaspoons salt
1 teaspoon parsley
2 tablespoons chopped celery leaves
2 carrots, diced
2 medium potatoes, cubed
2 stalks celery, diced
6-ounce can tomato paste
1 can cream-style corn
1/4 to 1/2 teaspoon poultry seasoning

Place chicken wings in a 2 ½-quart heavy saucepan with the chicken broth, 1 teaspoon of the salt, the parsley, and the celery leaves. Cover and simmer for 15 minutes. Add the carrots, potatoes, celery, and remaining salt. Simmer for 15 to 20 minutes, until the chicken and vegetables are tender. Add the tomato paste, corn, and poultry seasoning; mix well. Simmer, stirring, until heated through and slightly thickened.

October 1979
Oklahoma Rural News

Nacho Cheese Chowder

1 pound ground beef
1 small onion, chopped
1/2 green bell pepper, chopped
1 can whole corn, drained
1 can nacho cheese soup
1 can cream of mushroom soup
1 can diced tomatoes and green chilies, such as Rotel, undrained
1/2 cup milk

To a large pot, add the ground beef, onion, and bell pepper. Cook until the ground beef is browned; drain. Add the remaining ingredients and heat until hot.

Mrs. Charles Kerfoot
Perry, Okla.
Canadian Valley and Kay Electric Cooperatives

Cheesy Chicken Chowder

5 chicken breasts
6 to 8 potatoes, peeled and diced
1 small onion, chopped
¾ pound processed American cheese, such as Velveeta, cubed
5-ounce can evaporated milk, such as Milnot
1 can whole kernel corn
salt and black pepper, to taste

Place the chicken in a large pot, cover it with water, and cook. Once the chicken is cooked through, remove it from the pot. Add the potatoes and onion to the cooking liquid. While the potatoes are cooking, dice the chicken. When the potatoes are done, add the diced chicken and the remaining ingredients to the pot. Simmer for 30 minutes.

Helen Stangl
Perry, Okla.
Central Rural Electric Cooperative

PRACTICE GOOD EATING HABITS

Your chances of being happy and healthy at 65 or 70 will be greater if you make a strong ally of food all of your life—and not just when you're a child and mother makes you. Three major needs of the body supplied by food must be continuously replenished.

All through life you need food that contains protein and minerals, for they are the nutrients needed for the "upkeep" of body tissues and bone. Just as your home needs some repair work continually, so does your body. If the right materials are skimpy, the repairs might be shoddy.

Vitamins are the second basic need of your body, no matter what its age. Vitamins working with minerals and proteins make combination teams that keep the body running smoothly.

A third need supplied to the body from food is fuel for energy and warmth. All foods supply calories though some more than others. One problem, particularly among older persons, is getting calorie surplus, which leads to overweight.

Adequate amounts of milk, meat, eggs, fruit and vegetables, whole grain or enriched bread and cereals, and butter or fortified margarine would normally meet the body's needs for proteins, vitamins and minerals and fuel for energy. Beware of food fads and so-called wonder diets, which over-emphasize some foods and ignore others that are important.

Oklahoma Rural News
January 1954

Uniquely Oklahoman

Goobers

"Goobers" were first introduced to future Oklahoma, according to folklore, by the Cherokees in 1834–1835, when they were forced off their Georgia-Carolina farms and moved to Indian Territory. Now, 150 years later, we celebrate National Peanut Month in March with a proclamation to this effect issued by Governor George Nigh.

One of the most unique and delicious recipes to come out of traditional Oklahoma cookery is Cream of Peanut Soup. Based on chicken broth, to which onions and celery are added, the cream soup is subtly flavored with peanut butter. It makes an elegant first course which is simple to prepare.

Congressmen from Oklahoma recently introduced Cream of Peanut Soup and a superb dessert, Frozen Peanut Butter Pie (recipe on page 171), in the House of Representatives dining room in Washington. Both recipes were received enthusiastically by congressmen from all regions each time the soup and pie were featured on the House Restaurant menu.

Cream of Peanut Soup

¼ cup butter
1 cup thinly sliced celery
1 medium onion, chopped
2 tablespoons all-purpose flour
2 quarts chicken stock or broth
1 cup creamy peanut butter
1 cup light cream

Melt the butter in a large saucepan over low heat and add celery and onion. Cook until tender but not browned. Add flour and stir until the mixture is smooth. Gradually add chicken broth and bring to a boil. Blend in the peanut butter and simmer for about 15 minutes. Stir in cream just before serving.

March 1984
Oklahoma Rural News

Salads

Asparagus Summer Salad (see page 77).

Cherry Party Salad

12-to-16-ounce container whipped topping, such as Cool Whip
1 can sweetened condensed milk
20-ounce can crushed pineapple, drained
1 cup flaked coconut
1 can cherry pie filling
1 cup miniature marshmallows
½ cup chopped pecans (optional)

Combine the whipped topping and condensed milk in a large bowl and chill for 1 hour. Add remaining ingredients. Stir well and refrigerate overnight.

Donna Franklin
Ada, Okla.
People's Electric Cooperative

Broccoli Salad

2 packages frozen broccoli
1 package frozen French-style green beans
1 cucumber, chopped
1 onion, chopped
1 package ranch dressing mix, such as Hidden Valley

Prepare the broccoli and green beans separately according to package directions; chill. Combine the vegetables in a salad bowl. Mix the ranch dressing according to package directions and toss with the salad using the amount desired.

Romona White
Sayre, Okla.
Northfork Electric Cooperative

Asparagus Summer Salad

1 pound fresh asparagus
2 tablespoons canola oil
½ teaspoon salt
½ teaspoon black pepper
6 ounces salad mix
1 cucumber, sliced into thin rounds
12 strawberries, sliced
1 small red onion, sliced into thin rings
3 ounces feta cheese
balsamic vinaigrette dressing

Trim the ends of the asparagus and place asparagus in a 9-by-13-inch baking pan. Drizzle with oil and sprinkle with salt and pepper. Transfer the asparagus to a grill heated to medium-high (425°F). Cook for approximately 12 minutes, turning after 8 minutes, until the asparagus is lightly browned. Remove the asparagus from the grill and allow it to cool. Arrange the salad mix, cucumber slices, grilled asparagus, strawberries, and red onion in a serving bowl or individual bowls. Crumble feta cheese over the top. Dress the salad just before serving.

August 2012
Oklahoma Living

Johnny's Chicken Salad

Johnny's Chicken Salad

8 ounces cooked chicken
salt and white pepper
ground mustard
celery seeds
1 to 2 stalks celery, finely chopped
⅛ cup finely chopped pickles
⅛ cup sliced grapes
⅛ cup finely chopped pecans or almonds
⅛ cup cran-raisins
1 teaspoon mustard
2 to 3 tablespoons mayonnaise

Shred the chicken with a fork and season it with salt, white pepper, ground mustard, and celery seeds. Combine the celery, pickles, grapes, and pecans or almonds; add to the chicken. Add cran-raisins. Stir in the mustard and mayonnaise. Mix well. Serve on toasted bread.

Johnny Kerns
Fort Gibson, Okla.
Lake Region Electric Cooperative

Double Orange Gelatin Salad

"This is a family recipe from my mom. She loved orange sherbet and how cool and refreshing it was to serve for our summer Sunday dinners back in the 1940s and '50s in Owasso."

1 family-size package orange gelatin
2 cups boiling water
1 quart orange sherbet, such as Blue Bell
2 cans mandarin oranges, drained
2 cans crushed pineapple, drained
1 cup miniature marshmallows
3 large bananas, cut into bite-size pieces

Dissolve the gelatin in 2 cups of boiling water. Allow it to stand at room temperature for 15 minutes. Cut in the sherbet and fold in all remaining ingredients. Allow salad to set up in refrigerator for approximately 4 hours.

Nancy Jean Breckenridge
Talala, Okla.
Verdigris Valley Electric Cooperative

Uniquely Oklahoman

Aunt Florrie's Cornbread Salad

8 ½-ounce package cornbread mix
1 egg
⅓ cup milk
4 medium tomatoes, chopped
1 medium onion, chopped
½ pound bacon, fried and crumbled
½ cup chopped sweet pickles
½ green bell pepper, chopped
1 cup mayonnaise
¼ cup sweet pickle juice
1 cup shredded cheddar cheese

Preheat the oven to 400°F. Combine the cornbread mix, egg, and milk and spoon into a greased 8-inch pan. Bake for 15 minutes or until brown. Cool and cut into cubes and set aside. In a bowl, combine the tomatoes, onion, bacon, pickles, and bell pepper and toss gently. Combine mayonnaise and pickle juice. Layer half of the cornbread in a glass bowl. Add a layer of the tomato mixture and a layer of the mayonnaise mixture. Repeat layers. Sprinkle with cheese and chill for 2 hours.

Judith Whelchel
Blanchard, Okla.
Oklahoma Electric Cooperative

24-Hour Layer Salad

1 head lettuce
1 cup thinly sliced onion
1 cup thinly sliced celery
1 green bell pepper, thinly sliced
6-ounce can sliced water chestnuts
10-ounce package frozen peas
2 cups mayonnaise
1 teaspoon granulated sugar
½ teaspoon salt
½ teaspoon black pepper
1 cup shredded mozzarella cheese
½ cup grated Parmesan cheese

Shred the lettuce and place in the bottom of a 9-by-13-inch dish. Layer the onion, celery, bell pepper, and water chestnuts. Sprinkle with a layer of frozen peas and spread with a layer of mayonnaise. Sprinkle with a mixture of sugar, salt, and pepper. Top with both cheeses and cover tightly. Refrigerate for 24 hours or overnight. To make it a main dish, add one layer of thinly sliced ham or chicken.

Sonja Lowe
Carnegie, Okla.
Caddo Electric Cooperative

Grilled Corn, Avocado, and Tomato Salad with Honey-Lime Dressing

For the salad:
2 ears fresh sweet corn, husked
1 pint grape tomatoes, halved
1 avocado, diced
2 tablespoons chopped fresh cilantro

For the dressing:
1 lime, juiced
3 tablespoons vegetable oil
1 tablespoon honey
1 clove garlic, minced
salt and black pepper
dash cayenne pepper

Grill the corn over medium heat until it is tender but not mushy, about 10 minutes. Remove the corn from the cob and set it aside to cool. In a small bowl, whisk together the dressing ingredients. In a medium bowl, combine the corn, tomatoes, avocado, and cilantro. Add the dressing and toss gently to coat. Refrigerate for 15 minutes before serving.

Novell Wilson
Tulsa, Okla.
Verdigris Valley Electric Cooperative

Chicken and Veggie Salad

1 can corn, drained
1 can peas, drained
2 cups chopped Napa cabbage
⅓ cup chopped green onions
1 clove garlic, minced
1 ½ cups cooked and cubed seasoned chicken
¾ cup mayonnaise
salt and black pepper, to taste

Combine all ingredients in a medium bowl. Refrigerate for 1 hour before serving.

Stacey Foster
Crescent, Okla.
Cimarron Electric Cooperative

Stir-fried Beef and Grain Salad

Stir-fried Beef and Grain Salad

½ cup ready-to-cook couscous
¾ cup boiling water
1 pound beef strips
¾ teaspoon Italian seasoning
½ teaspoon lemon pepper seasoning
2 teaspoons vegetable oil
1 medium tomato, chopped
2 ½ tablespoons chopped parsley
2 tablespoons thinly sliced green onion
½ teaspoon salt

Combine the couscous and boiling water; cover and let stand for 15 minutes. Cool and crumble with fingers. Meanwhile, heat a nonstick frying pan over medium-high for 5 minutes. Sprinkle the beef strips with ½ teaspoon of the Italian seasoning and the lemon pepper seasoning. Add the oil to the frying pan and cook the beef strips over medium-high heat for 1 to 2 minutes or until beef is no longer pink. Combine the couscous with tomato, 2 tablespoons of the parsley, the green onion, the salt, and the remaining ¼ teaspoon of Italian seasoning. To serve, place couscous mixture on a serving platter and top with beef strips. Sprinkle with the remaining chopped parsley.

January 1991
Oklahoma Rural News

Broccoli-Cranberry Salad

Broccoli-Cranberry Salad

4 cups fresh bite-size broccoli florets
1 cup dried cranberries
½ cup diced red onion
½ cup cooked, crumbled bacon
½ cup mayonnaise
½ cup half-and-half
3 tablespoons granulated sugar

In a medium bowl, combine the broccoli florets, cranberries, onion, and bacon. In a small bowl, mix the mayonnaise, half-and-half, and sugar until smooth. Pour over the broccoli mixture and toss to coat. Refrigerate before serving.

Reta Bowen
Asher, Okla.
Canadian Valley Electric Cooperative

Grandma's Corned Beef Salad

2 3-ounce packages lemon-flavored gelatin, such as Jell-O
1 ¼ cups hot water
¼ cup granulated sugar
¼ cup vinegar
1 cup salad dressing, such as Miracle Whip
¼ teaspoon salt
1 tablespoon finely chopped green bell pepper
1 tablespoon finely chopped onion
1 cup chopped celery
3 hard-boiled eggs, chopped
12-ounce can corned beef, shredded

Dissolve the gelatin in hot water; let cool. Mix the sugar, vinegar, salad dressing, and salt together. Add the bell pepper, onion, celery, eggs, and corned beef to the mixture. Add the gelatin and chill until completely set.

Jacque Broadfoot
Beaver, Okla.
Tri-County Electric Cooperative

Chopped Summer Salad

For the salad:
1 ear corn, husked
1 orange bell pepper
1 tablespoon olive oil
1 large tomato
1 avocado
1 cucumber
¼ cup finely chopped red onion
1 cup cooked black beans
¼ cup chopped cilantro

For the dressing:
1 clove garlic
2 tablespoons lime juice
2 tablespoons orange juice
1 tablespoon honey
1 teaspoon ground cumin
3 tablespoons olive oil
salt and black pepper, to taste

Preheat the oven to 425°F. Coat the corn and bell pepper with olive oil and place on a baking sheet. Roast for about 20 minutes or until they start to brown, flipping them a few times as they cook. Let cool. Remove the corn from the cob and dice the bell pepper, along with the tomato, avocado, and cucumber, into ¼-inch pieces. Arrange the corn, bell pepper, tomato, avocado, cucumber, red onion, and black beans in separate piles on a platter. Sprinkle the chopped cilantro over the top. For the dressing, mince the garlic as finely as possible, or grate it with a fine grater into a small bowl. Add the lime juice, orange juice, honey, and cumin. Whisk in the olive oil and add salt and pepper to taste. Dress the salad just before serving.

June 2011
Oklahoma Living

Chopped Summer Salad

Tomato, Basil, and Fresh Mozzarella Salad

Tomato, Basil, and Fresh Mozzarella Salad

2 cups cherry tomatoes
¼ cup basil leaves
8 ounces fresh pearl mozzarella
2 tablespoons olive oil
1 tablespoon balsamic vinegar
salt and black pepper, to taste

Halve the cherry tomatoes. Chop or tear the basil leaves into small pieces. Place the tomatoes, basil, and mozzarella cheese into a serving bowl. Dress with the olive oil and vinegar immediately before serving. Season with salt and pepper to taste.

August 2011
Oklahoma Living

Delta's Funeral Salad

4 cans whole kernel corn, drained
1 cup chopped bell pepper
1 cup chopped onion
1 large jar pimientos
1 cup sliced green olives
1 large bottle Italian salad dressing
salt and black pepper, to taste

Mix the corn, bell pepper, onion, pimientos, and olives together in a large bowl. Stir in the salad dressing and season with salt and pepper to taste.

Delta Moffat
Lexington, Okla.
Oklahoma Electric Cooperative

Dee's Cranberry Salad

1 pound raw cranberries
2 cups granulated sugar
6-ounce package dark-colored gelatin
2 ⅔ cups boiling water
1 cup chopped nuts
1 can crushed pineapple, drained well

With a hand grinder or in a food processor, grind the cranberries and mix with sugar. Let stand in the refrigerator for at least 2 hours. Mix gelatin with boiling water and allow it to cool to room temperature. Stir in the cranberries, then add nuts and pineapple. Mix well and pour into a serving bowl or mold. Chill overnight before serving.

Barbara Harris
Pocola, Okla.
Arkansas Valley Electric Cooperative

Gelatin Pretzel Salad

2 cups crushed pretzels
3 tablespoons granulated sugar
¾ cup butter, melted
8 ounces cream cheese, softened
1 large container whipped topping, such as Cool Whip
½ cup powdered sugar
2 cups miniature marshmallows
1 large package strawberry-flavored gelatin, such as Jell-O
2 cups boiling water
12-ounce package frozen strawberries

Preheat the oven to 350°F. Mix together the pretzels, sugar, and butter and press into the bottom of a 9-by-13-inch baking pan. Bake for 15 minutes and cool completely. Fold the cream cheese, whipped topping, powdered sugar, and marshmallows together and spoon over the top of the crust. Dissolve the gelatin in boiling water, add strawberries, and stir until strawberries are thawed. Place the mixture in the freezer for about 15 minutes until thickened but not completely set. Spread it on top of the base layer and chill until completely set.

Patricia Babcock
Kingston, Okla.
Red River Valley Rural Electric Association

Raw Cranberry Relish

"This makes a large amount. It will keep through the holiday season and gets better as it ages. It is good with the turkey, of course, but also with most meats and poultry. My husband uses it as the fruit for his weekend muffins—gently stir a half cup or so into the batter at the last moment so that it doesn't turn the batter bright pink."

2 12-ounce bags fresh cranberries
2 oranges, peeled
2 crisp red apples or pears, cored but not peeled
2 packages cranberry- or raspberry-flavored gelatin, such as Jell-O
1 cup white wine or fruit juice
½ cup chopped walnuts
1 cup granulated sugar

To a food processor, gradually add all fruit and coarsely chop after each addition. In a large bowl, combine all ingredients and mix well. Refrigerate for at least 24 hours before serving.

Lin Archer
Harrah, Okla.
Oklahoma Electric Cooperative

Ginger Pear Mold

1 package raspberry-flavored gelatin
½ cup hot water
1 ½ teaspoons lemon juice
1 ½ cups ginger ale
1 cup fresh pears, diced

Dissolve the gelatin in hot water. Add the lemon juice and ginger ale gradually. Chill until slightly thickened but not completely set. Fold in the pears and turn into a 1-quart mold. Chill until firm. Remove from the mold and garnish with pear quarters, grape clusters, and green leaves.

September 1950
Oklahoma Rural News

Ginger Pear Mold

Uniquely Oklahoman

Pickled Black-eyed Peas

2 cans black-eyed peas
¾ cup Italian dressing, such as Wishbone
½ cup cider vinegar
garlic seasoning
½ cup thinly sliced green onion
½ teaspoon salt
cracked or freshly ground black pepper
dash hot sauce, such as Tabasco

Drain the liquid from the peas and place them in a bowl. Add remaining ingredients and mix thoroughly. Store in refrigerator at least 2 days before serving.

Frances H. Gardner
Bartlesville, Okla.
Verdigris Valley Electric Cooperative

Lemony Orzo Salad

1 cup uncooked orzo pasta
1 ⅓ cups diced zucchini
⅓ cup diced red onion
⅓ cup minced fresh parsley
3 tablespoons fresh lemon juice
1 tablespoon minced fresh (or 1 teaspoon dried) basil
1 tablespoon olive oil
2 teaspoons minced fresh mint
½ teaspoon salt
¼ teaspoon black pepper
1 cup diced tomato
⅓ cup (1 ½ ounces) crumbled feta cheese
2 tablespoons chopped and pitted kalamata olives

Cook the orzo according to package directions, omitting salt and fat. Drain well. Combine the orzo, zucchini, and onion in a large bowl; toss well. Combine the parsley, lemon juice, basil, oil, mint, salt, and pepper with a whisk. Stir into the orzo mixture. Add the tomato, cheese, and olives, tossing gently to coat.

Michelle Lawson
Perry, Okla.
Central Rural Electric Cooperative

Sides

Toasted Quinoa (see page 94).

Ola Manns' Mac and Cheese

"'Mama Ola' has made this dish for many years. It is the best old-school mac and cheese ever and the most requested dish at all family gatherings."

½ pound elbow macaroni
1 can evaporated milk, such as Milnot
2 tablespoons butter
½ teaspoon salt
1 egg, beaten
4 ½ cups shredded mild cheddar cheese

Preheat the oven to 375°F. In a large pot, cook the pasta according to package directions. As the pasta is boiling, prepare the cheese sauce. To a large saucepan over low heat, add the evaporated milk, butter, and salt. Gradually stir in the egg. Add 4 cups of the cheese and gradually increase the heat to medium until cheese is melted. Drain the noodles. Stir the cheese sauce into the pot with the pasta. Pour the mixture into a greased 9-by-13-inch glass baking dish. Top with the remaining ½ cup of cheese. Bake for approximately 20 minutes or until the top is slightly browned.

Sheila Anderson
Lawton, Okla.

King Ranch Chicken Mac and Cheese

8 ounces cellentani pasta
2 tablespoons butter
1 medium onion, diced
1 green bell pepper, diced
10-ounce can diced tomatoes and green chilies
8-ounce package processed American cheese, cubed
3 cups cooked and chopped chicken
10-ounce can cream of chicken soup
½ cup sour cream
1 teaspoon chili powder
½ teaspoon ground cumin
1 ½ cups shredded cheddar cheese

Preheat the oven to 350°F. Prepare the pasta according to package directions; drain. Meanwhile, melt the butter in a large pot or Dutch oven over medium-high heat. Add the onion and bell pepper and sauté for 5 minutes or until tender. Stir in the diced tomatoes and green chilies and American cheese. Cook, stirring constantly, for 2 minutes or until the cheese melts. Stir in the chicken, soup, sour cream, chili powder, and cumin. Add the cooked pasta and mix until blended. Spoon the mixture into a greased 10-inch cast-iron skillet or a 7-by-11-inch baking dish. Top with shredded cheddar cheese. Bake for 30 minutes or until bubbly.

Regina Waugh
Cherokee, Okla.
Alfalfa Electric Cooperative

Scalloped Corn

"This is my husband's absolute favorite vegetable dish."

½ green bell pepper, chopped
1 small onion, minced
2 tablespoons butter
2 tablespoons all-purpose flour
1 cup milk
2 cans whole kernel corn, drained
1 small jar pimientos, chopped
1 teaspoon salt
1 teaspoon granulated sugar
½ teaspoon dry mustard
dash cayenne pepper
2 eggs, beaten
⅓ cup breadcrumbs

Preheat the oven to 350°F. In a skillet over low heat, sauté the bell pepper and onion in butter. Add the flour and mix well. Add the milk and continue cooking over low heat, stirring until thickened. Add the corn, pimientos, salt, sugar, mustard, and pepper. Remove from the heat and stir in the eggs. Transfer to a greased baking dish and cover with buttered breadcrumbs. Bake until crumbs are browned and mixture is bubbly hot, about 30 minutes.

Reta Bowen
Asher, Okla.
Canadian Valley Electric Cooperative

Parmesan-Rosemary Potatoes

3 pounds baking potatoes
3 cups cold water
2 teaspoons salt
1 cup finely shredded Parmesan cheese
½ cup fine, dry breadcrumbs
2 ½ tablespoons finely chopped
fresh rosemary
1 teaspoon salt
½ teaspoon garlic powder
¼ teaspoon black pepper
1 cup butter, melted

Preheat the oven to 400°F. Wash the potatoes. Cut them in half lengthwise, then crosswise into half moon-shaped wedges. Combine the water and 1 teaspoon of the salt in a large bowl. Add the potatoes and allow them to soak for 5 minutes. Meanwhile, combine the cheese, breadcrumbs, rosemary, remaining teaspoon of salt, garlic powder, and pepper in a small bowl. After the potatoes have soaked, drain them well and spread them on paper towels or clean kitchen towels and pat dry. Dip the potato wedges in butter and roll them in the Parmesan mixture to coat evenly. Arrange wedges in a single layer on a lightly greased baking sheet. Bake for 40 minutes or until potatoes are tender and golden brown. Sprinkle lightly with salt before serving. Garnish with fresh rosemary.

Kay Bamberl
Monkey Island, Okla.
Northeast Oklahoma Electric Cooperative

Herbed Onion Scalloped Potatoes

5 large potatoes, peeled and thinly sliced
¾ cup chopped onion
3 tablespoons butter
¼ cup all-purpose flour
1 ¾ cups low-sodium chicken broth
2 tablespoons mayonnaise
2 cloves garlic, minced
¾ teaspoon salt
¼ teaspoon dried parsley
¼ teaspoon poultry seasoning
⅛ teaspoon black pepper
¼ cup chopped fresh chives

Preheat the oven to 325°F. Grease a 2 ½-quart baking dish. Layer the potatoes and onion in the prepared baking dish. Melt the butter in a saucepan over medium heat; stir in the flour until smooth. Gradually add the broth, mayonnaise, garlic, salt, parsley, poultry seasoning, and pepper; cook and stir until thick and bubbly, about 2 minutes. Pour the mayonnaise mixture over the potatoes and onion. Cover the baking dish with foil. Bake until potatoes are tender, about 1 hour and 45 minutes. Remove the foil and continue to bake until golden brown on top, about 15 minutes more. Sprinkle with chives to serve.

Mary J. Moerbe
Blackwell, Okla.
Kay Electric Cooperative

Uniquely Oklahoman

Ham 'n' Beans

1 pound dried Great Northern beans
6 slices bacon
½ large onion, diced
16 ounces ham, diced
3 cans chicken broth
1 ½ tablespoons garlic powder
1 tablespoon onion powder
1 teaspoon black pepper
2 tablespoons dried parsley
1 ½ teaspoons salt

Soak the beans overnight in water; drain. In a large skillet, fry the bacon until crisp, then remove it from the skillet and crumble. Add the onion and ham to the bacon grease in the skillet and sauté until browned. Add the beans, bacon, ham mixture, broth, garlic powder, onion powder, pepper, and parsley to a slow cooker. Cook on low for 8 hours. Add salt before serving.

Sandra Hook
Norman, Okla.
Oklahoma Electric Cooperative

Really Good Baked Beans

4 cans pork and beans
½ cup chopped green bell pepper
1 cup chopped onion
½ cup brown sugar
½ teaspoon oregano
½ teaspoon dry mustard
½ teaspoon black pepper
1 small can tomato sauce
½ cup ketchup
bacon

Preheat the oven to 325°F. Mix all ingredients and top with bacon. Pour into a greased 9-by-13-inch baking dish. Bake uncovered until bubbly.

Rachel Meredith
Sallisaw, Okla.
Cookson Hills Electric Cooperative

Corn Fritters

1 ½ cups all-purpose flour
¾ teaspoon baking powder
1 ½ teaspoons salt
2 eggs, beaten
½ cup milk
2 cups whole kernel corn
oil for frying

Sift the flour, measure it, and resift it into a medium bowl, along with the baking powder and salt. Stir in the eggs and milk and mix until smooth. Fold in the corn. Drop teaspoons of the batter into oil heated in a saucepan to 375°F. Fry until golden, remove from the oil, and drain on paper towels. Serve with syrup if desired.

August 1995
Oklahoma Living

Uniquely Oklahoman

Fried Hominy

2 strips bacon
2 to 3 green onions
2 cups hominy

In a skillet over medium heat, fry the bacon; drain. Cut the green onions into small pieces. Crumble the bacon and add it back to the skillet along with the onions. When the onions begin to fry, add the hominy and cook for 10 to 15 minutes, first on high heat, then on low.

The Cherokee Nation

Texhoma Beans

1 pound ground beef
1 onion, chopped
1 teaspoon chopped garlic
½ package taco seasoning
1 can diced tomatoes and green chilies, such as Rotel
½ teaspoon ground cumin
½ teaspoon garlic powder
½ teaspoon oregano
1 tablespoon chili powder (optional)
1 pound pinto beans, cooked and seasoned with salt and bacon

In a large skillet, brown the ground beef with the onion and garlic; drain. Add the taco seasoning, diced tomatoes and green chilies, and spices. Add the beef mixture to the beans and simmer together for about 30 minutes. Serve with rice.

Jan Miles
Coalgate, Okla.
People's Electric Cooperative

Double-Baked Potato Casserole

3 pounds (about 8 large) potatoes, cut into 1-inch cubes
½ cup butter
1 cup sour cream
2 teaspoons seasoned salt
1 teaspoon black pepper
4 green onions, chopped
8 slices bacon, cooked and crumbled
1 cup shredded cheese

Cover the potatoes with water in a large saucepan. Bring to a boil over medium-high heat. Reduce the heat and simmer, covered, until tender, about 20 to 25 minutes. Preheat the oven to 350°F. Grease a 9-by-13-inch baking dish. Drain the potatoes and transfer them to a large bowl. Add the butter, sour cream, salt, and pepper. Mash the potato mixture with a potato masher until well blended. If the mixture seems dry, add an additional 3 to 4 tablespoons of sour cream and 2 tablespoons of butter. Stir in the green onions, bacon, and cheese. Spoon into the prepared dish and bake, uncovered, for about 25 minutes.

Reta Bowen
Asher, Okla.
Canadian Valley Electric Cooperative

Hash Brown Potato Casserole

32-ounce bag shredded hash brown potatoes, thawed
4 to 5 slices bacon, cooked and crumbled
1 cup butter or margarine, melted
1 can cream of chicken soup
12 ounces shredded American cheese
8 ounces sour cream
1 teaspoon salt
1 teaspoon black pepper
½ small onion, chopped and sautéed
2 cups crushed corn flakes

Preheat the oven to 350°F. Place the potatoes in a greased 9-by-13-inch baking dish. Mix the bacon, ½ cup of the butter or margarine, soup, cheese, sour cream, salt, pepper, and onion and layer over the potatoes. Top with crushed corn flakes. Drizzle the remaining ½ cup of butter or margarine over the top. Bake, uncovered, for 45 minutes.

John Long
Sand Springs, Okla.
Indian Electric Cooperative

Toasted Quinoa

2 teaspoons olive oil
2 teaspoons white miso paste
1 cup quinoa, rinsed
2 cups water
green onions

To a medium saucepan, add the olive oil, miso paste, and quinoa and stir. Cook the quinoa over medium heat, stirring frequently, for 5 minutes or until the quinoa is golden. Add the water. Once the water boils, reduce the heat to low and cover the saucepan. Cook for 15 minutes. Fluff the quinoa with a fork. Serve with finely chopped green onions.

June 2012
Oklahoma Living

Mother's Black-eyed Peas

3 slices salt pork
1 to 2 cups dried black-eyed peas, rinsed
1 onion, chopped
3 stalks celery, chopped
1 to 3 jalapeño peppers
1 can tomatoes
1 small can tomato sauce
bacon grease

In a pot, boil the salt pork in 1 quart of water for 30 minutes. Add the peas, onion, celery, and whole jalapeños. Cook for 1 hour or until the peas are tender. If needed, add more water to keep the peas covered. When the peas are done, remove the peppers and add the tomatoes and tomato sauce. Season with bacon grease, if desired.

Mary Louise Nix
Duncan, Okla.
Cotton Electric Cooperative

Praline Sweet Potato Casserole

- 3 cups fresh sweet potatoes, cooked and mashed, or 3 15-ounce cans, heated and mashed
- ½ cup unsalted butter
- 1 cup granulated sugar
- 1 teaspoon vanilla extract
- ½ cup milk
- 2 eggs, beaten
- ½ cup light brown sugar
- ⅓ cup all-purpose flour
- ½ cup chopped pecans

Preheat the oven to 350°F. Combine the mashed sweet potatoes and ¼ cup of the butter; mix until butter is melted. Add the granulated sugar, vanilla, and milk. Stir in the eggs and mix well. Transfer to a 9-by-13-inch glass baking dish. In a small bowl, combine the brown sugar and flour. Cut in the remaining ¼ cup of butter until crumbly. Stir in the pecans. Sprinkle over the top of the sweet potato mixture. Bake for 35 to 45 minutes, until the topping is browned. Serve hot. The casserole can be made a day in advance and refrigerated. Allow it to come to room temperature, about 30 minutes, before baking.

Jackie Brooks
Kansas, Okla.
Northeast Oklahoma Electric Cooperative

FREEZE THOSE GARDEN-FRESH VEGETABLES NOW FOR DELICIOUS OUT-OF-SEASON DINNER TREATS

Thousands of homemakers all over the country are finding a home freezer one of their most cherished possessions. They are finding that they can preserve almost every kind of food for periods of time ranging from several months to a year or more by freezing.

That means good eating the year 'round for the entire family. It means also that the homemaker's work is reduced by many hours in the course of the year, because freezing foods, whether they be fruits, vegetables, meats or bakery products, requires less time than other means of preserving. Also—no amount of fresh produce is too small to freeze, even a box or two, whereas no housewife would think of going through the hot canning process for only a pint of food.

Since this is the time of year our gardens are generously yielding an abundance of wholesome, colorful fresh vegetables, let's discuss freezing of vegetables for next winter's dinners.

Oklahoma Rural News
June 1949

Vegetables are blanched before being frozen for future use. The electric freezer allowed families access to nutritious produce year-round.

Sweet Carrot Casserole

1 pound carrots
1 cup water
6 tablespoons butter or margarine, melted
2 tablespoons all-purpose flour
1 teaspoon baking powder
½ cup granulated sugar
3 eggs
1 teaspoon vanilla extract

Preheat the oven to 350°F. Peel the carrots and cut them in chunks. Place them in a saucepan with the water and cook until tender. Drain the carrots and mash them with a potato masher. Stir in the butter. Add the remaining ingredients and blend together with an electric mixer. Pour the carrots into a greased 9-inch-square baking dish. Bake for 45 minutes.

Elaine Rose Hrdy-Straka
Oklahoma City, Okla.
Oklahoma Electric Cooperative

Zucchini Patties

2 cups shredded zucchini
⅓ cup biscuit mix
½ cup shredded cheddar cheese
2 tablespoons grated onion
½ teaspoon dried basil
½ teaspoon salt
¼ teaspoon black pepper
2 eggs, beaten
2 tablespoons butter or margarine

Combine the zucchini, biscuit mix, cheese, onion, basil, salt, and pepper in a large bowl; mix well. Stir in the eggs and mix well. Shape the batter into six ¼-cup patties. In a skillet, melt the butter. Cook the patties in the butter for 4 to 5 minutes or until lightly browned on each side.

S. Francie Russell
Meeker, Okla.
Canadian Valley Electric Cooperative

Best-Ever Broccoli Casserole

1 large head of fresh broccoli or 16-ounce package frozen broccoli florets
1 can cream of chicken or cream of mushroom soup
½ cup butter
1 sleeve saltine crackers, crushed
1 to 1 ½ cups shredded cheddar cheese

Preheat the oven to 350°F. Steam the broccoli until tender; drain the liquid. In a bowl, mix the broccoli with the cream soup. Place the butter in an 8-by-11-inch baking dish and place it into the oven until it melts. Sprinkle the crushed crackers over the butter and mix. Spread the broccoli mixture over the buttered crackers. Top with the cheese. Bake until heated through.

Rachel Meredith
Sallisaw, Okla.
Cookson Hills Electric Cooperative

Butterscotch Yams

6 medium yams, cooked, peeled, and quartered
½ cup corn syrup
½ cup packed brown sugar
¼ cup heavy cream or half-and-half
2 tablespoons margarine
½ teaspoon salt
½ teaspoon ground cinnamon

Preheat the oven to 325°F. Arrange the yams in a single layer in a 9-by-13-inch baking dish. Bake for 15 minutes. In a 2-quart saucepan, combine the remaining ingredients. Bring the contents to a boil over medium heat, stirring constantly. Boil for 5 minutes. Pour the mixture over the yams. Bake for 15 minutes, basting frequently.

November 1994
Oklahoma Living

Roasted Country Vegetables

⅓ cup olive oil
1 teaspoon garlic powder
1 teaspoon salt
½ teaspoon black pepper
1 head cauliflower, cut into florets
1 red bell pepper, cut into 1-inch chunks
1 onion, peeled and cut into 1-inch chunks
3 carrots, peeled and cut into 1-inch chunks

Preheat the oven to 425°F. Coat a rimmed baking sheet with cooking spray. In a large bowl, combine the oil, garlic powder, salt, and pepper; mix well. Add the vegetables to the bowl, tossing until evenly coated. Place on the prepared baking sheet. Roast for 30 to 35 minutes or until tender.

Sue Young
Ada, Okla.
People's Electric Cooperative

Eggplant-Zucchini Ratatouille

1 medium eggplant, unpeeled
1 ½ teaspoons salt
1 large onion, thinly sliced
1 large green bell pepper, chopped
2 cloves garlic, minced
2 tablespoons vegetable oil
3 medium zucchini, sliced
3 tomatoes, peeled and chopped
⅛ teaspoon black pepper
1 teaspoon dried oregano
2 tablespoons chopped fresh parsley
2 to 4 tablespoons grated Parmesan cheese (optional)

Cut the eggplant into cubes and cover with cold water and 1 teaspoon of the salt. Set aside for about 20 minutes. In a large skillet, sauté the onion, bell pepper, and garlic in hot oil until vegetables are crisp-tender. Stir in the eggplant and zucchini; cook for 5 minutes. Add the tomatoes, remaining ½ teaspoon of salt, pepper, oregano, and parsley. Stir well and cook until heated through. Pour into a serving bowl and sprinkle with cheese if desired.

Lydia L. Roper
Caddo, Okla.
Southeastern Electric Cooperative

Savory Fresh Mushrooms

2 pounds fresh mushrooms
¼ cup dry sherry
2 teaspoons butter or margarine
½ teaspoon paprika
½ teaspoon seasoned salt
¼ teaspoon black pepper
½ cup chopped fresh parsley

Combine all ingredients in a large skillet. Cover and cook over medium heat for 5 minutes, stirring occasionally.

November 1990
Oklahoma Rural News

Hearts 'n' Caps

16-ounce can unmarinated artichoke hearts, drained and quartered
½ cup grated Parmesan cheese
½ pound mushrooms, sliced
2 tablespoons butter
1 cup heavy cream

Preheat the oven to 350°F. Arrange the artichoke hearts in a greased 1 ½-quart baking dish. Sprinkle with ¼ cup of the Parmesan cheese. Sauté the mushrooms in butter in a medium skillet until tender. Add the cream. Cook over low heat until most of the cream is absorbed, stirring occasionally. Pour mushroom mixture over artichokes and sprinkle with the remaining ¼ cup of Parmesan cheese. Bake for 20 to 30 minutes.

Sandra Hook
Norman, Okla.
Oklahoma Electric Cooperative

APRIL IS THE MONTH FOR THE FARM HOMEMAKER TO:

1. Clean out the basement for summer use; clean, check storm cellar.
2. Teach the youngsters to milk.
3. Plot to keep insects out of the house.
4. Get garden insect spray supplies, but keep out of reach of youngsters.
5. Darn hubby's socks.
6. Serve iron content food to help cut down on "spring fever."
7. Don't overlook spring vegetables.

Oklahoma Rural News
April 1953

Sweet Potato-Apple Delight

1 can whole sweet potatoes
1 can apple slices, drained
¼ cup lemon juice
¼ cup honey

Preheat the oven to 350°F. Cut the sweet potatoes into ½-inch slices. Arrange alternating layers of sweet potatoes and apples in a baking pan. In a small bowl, combine the lemon juice and honey. Pour the mixture over the sweet potatoes and apples. Bake for 20 minutes or until heated through.

February 1968
Oklahoma Rural News

Shredded Brussels Sprouts with Pecans and Mustard Seeds

⅓ cup pecans, coarsely chopped
20 ounces Brussels sprouts, ends trimmed
½ tablespoon butter
2 teaspoons olive oil
1 tablespoon yellow mustard seeds
1 to 2 tablespoons fresh lemon juice
coarse salt and black pepper

Preheat the oven to 350°F. Spread the pecans on a rimmed baking sheet and toast until fragrant and lightly browned, about 10 minutes; set aside. Meanwhile, with the shredding disk of a food processor, shred the Brussels sprouts. Or, halve them and slice thinly with a knife. In a large nonstick skillet, heat the butter and oil over medium-high heat. Add the mustard seeds and cook, stirring occasionally, until fragrant, about 30 seconds. Add Brussels sprouts and cook, tossing occasionally until tender and beginning to brown, about 7 to 9 minutes. Remove from the heat, stir in the lemon juice, and season with salt and pepper. Serve topped with pecans.

Michelle Lawson
Perry, Okla.
Central Rural Electric Cooperative

Roasted Acorn Squash

2 acorn squash, peeled
⅓ cup vegetable oil
½ teaspoon salt
¼ teaspoon black pepper
¼ cup maple syrup

Preheat the oven to 400°F. Cut the tops off the acorn squash, slice in half, remove the seeds, and cut the halves into 2-inch chunks. In a large bowl, combine the oil, salt, and pepper; mix well. Add the squash to the oil mixture and toss to coat. Place the squash on a rimmed baking sheet and bake for 50 to 60 minutes or until tender. Drizzle with maple syrup and serve.

Sue Young
Ada, Okla.
People's Electric Cooperative

Sausage, Squash, and Pecan Casserole

For the casserole:

2 pounds yellow squash or zucchini, sliced
4 tablespoons butter
2 medium onions, sliced
1 clove garlic, minced
1 cup milk
1 cup breadcrumbs
1 pound sausage, cooked and crumbled
4 eggs, beaten
1 ½ cups shredded sharp cheddar cheese
1 cup chopped pecans
1 teaspoon salt
freshly ground black pepper

For the topping:

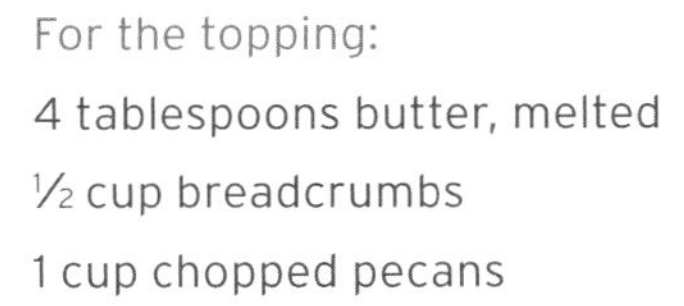

4 tablespoons butter, melted
½ cup breadcrumbs
1 cup chopped pecans

Preheat the oven to 350°F. Grease a 2-quart baking dish and set aside. Place the squash in a heavy pot and add enough water to cover. Bring to a boil, uncovered, then reduce the heat and simmer for 30 minutes or until squash is soft. Drain and mash. In a large skillet, melt the butter. Add the onion and garlic and cook until soft. Add the onion mixture to the squash. Heat the milk in the same skillet. Stir in the breadcrumbs and add the mixture to the squash. Stir in the sausage, eggs, cheese, pecans, salt, and pepper. Pour the mixture into the prepared baking dish. For the topping, combine the butter, breadcrumbs, and pecans and sprinkle over the casserole. Bake for 30 minutes.

March 1985
Oklahoma Rural News

Sausage, Squash, and Pecan Casserole

Broccoli Casserole

2 cups uncooked instant rice
10-ounce box chopped broccoli
½ onion, chopped
6 tablespoons butter
1 jar processed cheese sauce, such as Cheez Whiz
1 can cream of chicken soup

Preheat the oven to 300°F. Cook the rice and the broccoli according to their package directions. Sauté the onion in butter. Mix all ingredients together. Transfer to a greased 9-by-13-inch baking dish. Bake for 30 minutes.

Mary Ann Koehn
Fairview, Okla.
Cimarron Electric Cooperative

Sautéed Asparagus with Bacon

2 slices bacon
2 bunches (about 2 pounds) asparagus
coarse salt and freshly ground black pepper, to taste
2 teaspoons Dijon mustard
3 tablespoons chopped fresh parsley

In a large skillet, cook the bacon over medium heat until browned and crisp; drain. Cut the bacon into 1-inch pieces. Trim the asparagus ends. Cut the spears into 1- to 1 ½-inch pieces. Place the asparagus into the skillet with the bacon grease and season with salt and pepper to taste. Cook, stirring, until asparagus is tender, about 10 minutes. Remove from heat and stir in the bacon, Dijon mustard, and parsley. Serve hot.

Ruth Ann Hightower
Ralston, Okla.
Indian Electric Cooperative

German Sauerkraut

2 thick slices lean bacon
1 medium yellow onion, peeled and sliced
1 quart sauerkraut in a glass jar or fresh sauerkraut, rinsed and drained
1 cup peeled and grated potatoes
1 tablespoon brown sugar
1 cup dry white wine
1 bay leaf
2 teaspoons caraway seeds
black pepper, to taste

Place all ingredients in a heavy pot and simmer gently for 2 hours.

Clara Schrader
Oklahoma City, Okla.
Oklahoma Electric Cooperative

Herb-Roasted Tomatoes

Herb-Roasted Tomatoes

1 large tomato
1 teaspoon olive oil
¼ teaspoon dried basil
¼ teaspoon dried oregano
⅛ teaspoon salt
⅛ teaspoon black pepper
1 teaspoon Parmesan cheese

Preheat the oven to 350°F. Cut the tomato in half. Drizzle with oil and sprinkle with basil, oregano, salt, pepper, and Parmesan cheese. Bake until the tomato is heated through, approximately 20 minutes.

March 2013
Oklahoma Living

Sliced Zucchini Pickles

1 quart vinegar
2 cups granulated sugar
½ cup salt
2 teaspoons celery salt
2 teaspoons turmeric
1 teaspoon ground mustard
4 quarts sliced zucchini
1 quart sliced onions

Bring the vinegar, sugar, salt, and spices to a boil. Pour over the zucchini and onions and let stand for 1 hour. Then, heat to boiling and cook for 3 minutes. Pack in hot sterilized jars and seal.

September 1975
Oklahoma Rural News

A 1970s homemaker cans produce for later use. Prior to electricity, canning was an essential means of food preservation.

Pickled Peppers

6 to 7 red and/or green bell peppers
boiling water
1 ½ cups vinegar
3 cups granulated sugar

Wash, stem, seed, and slice the peppers. (Should yield 2 quarts.) Place the peppers in a large bowl and cover with boiling water. Let stand for 5 minutes. Drain well and place the pepper slices in sterilized ½-pint jars. Combine the vinegar and sugar in a saucepan; stir to dissolve sugar. Bring the mixture to a boil and simmer for 5 minutes. Pour the hot syrup over the peppers to fill jars to 1 inch from the top. Seal. Place the jars into a water bath and process for 5 minutes. Let stand for 4 weeks.

October 1974
Oklahoma Rural News

Main Dishes & Casseroles

Linguine with Tomatoes, Anchovies, and Capers *(see page 108).*

Four-Cheese Pasta Florentine

1 link precooked smoked sausage
3 cups uncooked mostaccioli or penne rigate pasta
5 ounces chopped frozen spinach
4 ounces cream cheese
1 cup small-curd cottage cheese
2 eggs, beaten
1 teaspoon minced garlic
2 to 3 ounces sliced ripe olives
8 ounces mozzarella cheese
¼ cup grated Parmesan cheese

Preheat the oven to 375°F. Slice the smoked sausage into thin slices. Cook the pasta according to package directions. Meanwhile, cook the spinach according to package directions; drain well. Place in a large bowl. Add the cream cheese; stir until melted. Stir in the cottage cheese, eggs, garlic, sausage, and olives. Drain the pasta and add it along with the mozzarella to the rest of the ingredients in the bowl; mix lightly. Spoon into a lightly oiled 10-inch-square baking dish and top with Parmesan cheese. Bake for 25 minutes or until heated through and lightly browned on top.

John Long
Sand Springs, Okla.
Indian Electric Cooperative

Pasta with Sausage and Peppers

16 ounces penne pasta
1 pound Polish sausage
2 tablespoons olive oil
1 small onion, julienned
1 green bell pepper, julienned

Cook the pasta according to package directions and drain. Slice the sausage into ¼-inch medallions. Cook the sausage in a skillet with the oil. Add the onions and bell pepper and cook until tender. Add the pasta and mix to coat with the oil in the pan.

Odus Hennessee
Medicine Park, Okla.
Cotton Electric Cooperative

Chicken Spaghetti

1 3-to-4-pound chicken
12 ounces spaghetti noodles
1 onion, chopped
1 bell pepper, chopped
½ cup chopped celery
¼ cup butter
1 can diced green chilies
1 can cream of mushroom soup
1 can cream of chicken soup
1 can cream of celery soup
1 can chicken broth
1 pound processed American cheese, such as Velveeta, cubed
salt and black pepper
garlic powder, to taste

Preheat the oven to 350°F. Boil the chicken until cooked through. Debone the chicken and cut it into small pieces. Cook spaghetti according to package directions. Sauté the onion, bell pepper, and celery in the butter until tender. Combine with the remaining ingredients and stir into the cooked spaghetti. Place the mixture in a greased 9-by-13-inch baking pan. Cover with foil and bake for 30 to 45 minutes or until thoroughly heated.

Donna Franklin
Ada, Okla.
People's Electric Cooperative

White Lasagna

1 small onion, chopped
¼ cup margarine
½ cup all-purpose flour
2 cups light cream
1 ½ cups chicken broth
¼ cup parsley
½ cup white wine (optional)
salt and black pepper, to taste
9 lasagna noodles, cooked
4 cups chopped or shredded cooked chicken
1 pound mozzarella cheese, cut into strips
¼ cup Parmesan cheese

Preheat the oven to 350°F. For the sauce, brown the onions in the margarine. Add the flour and cook until thickened. Add the cream and broth. Cook, stirring, until thick and bubbly. Add the parsley, wine, and the salt and pepper to taste. Set aside. Grease a 9-by-13-inch pan. Arrange 3 noodles on the bottom of the pan. Sprinkle 2 cups of the chicken over the top. Cover with a third of the sauce and a third of the cheese. Repeat the process until all of the ingredients are used up. Sprinkle the top with Parmesan cheese. Bake until hot and bubbly, about 20 minutes.

Lydia L. Roper
Caddo, Okla.
Southeastern Electric Cooperative

Crescent Dinner Roll Lasagna

"My sister shared this recipe with me back in the 1970s. This is my family's favorite lasagna. I've never seen it in any recipe book I own."

1 small carton cottage cheese
½ cup Parmesan cheese
3 eggs
1 pound sausage
2 pounds ground beef
1 onion, chopped
2 small cans tomato paste
1 small can tomato sauce
1 teaspoon garlic salt or powder
1 teaspoon salt
1 teaspoon black pepper
1 teaspoon oregano
½ teaspoon basil
½ teaspoon ground cumin
2 tubes crescent rolls
mozzarella cheese slices

Mix together the cottage cheese, Parmesan cheese, and eggs; set aside. Brown the sausage, ground beef, and onion; drain. To the meat mixture, add the tomato paste and tomato sauce; stir. Add all of the spices. In a greased 9-by-13-inch baking dish, unroll one tube of the crescent rolls. Press the crescent rolls together until the bottom of the pan is covered. Spread half of the hot meat mixture over the rolls. Cover with the cheese mixture. Spread the remaining meat over the cheese and lay the slices of mozzarella cheese on top. Press together a second can of crescent rolls and lay it over the top of the cheese. Bake according to crescent roll package directions, or until the top is browned.

Clauddea Austin
Owasso, Okla.
Verdigris Valley Electric Cooperative

ON EATING OUT

The cost of eating out has risen more than 10 percent over the past year.

Food away from home now accounts for nearly a third of your food dollar. Fast food outlets continue to grow most rapidly.

Meals at fast food restaurants usually cost considerably more than the same meals prepared at home. In addition, food prepared at home is frequently made from higher quality ingredients, e.g. more milk in milk shakes, or real ice cream in a sundae.

As a comparison, one quarter-pound hamburger will average 89 cents at a fast food place compared to 56 cents at home, and French fries will cost 39 cents and 15 cents respectively.

Oklahoma Rural News
August 1979

Easy Lasagna

1 pound ground beef
24-ounce jar spaghetti sauce, such as Ragu
5 lasagna noodles
½ pound Monterey jack or Colby cheese, shredded
½ pound mozzarella cheese, shredded

Preheat the oven to 350°F. Cook the ground beef and drain excess grease. Add the spaghetti sauce. Cook the lasagna noodles according to package directions. In a baking dish, layer the lasagna noodles, meat sauce, and cheeses. Repeat layers, using mozzarella cheese for the top layer. Bake until bubbly, about 25 to 30 minutes.

Catherine Fannin
Marietta, Okla.

Linguine with Tomatoes, Anchovies, and Capers

4 large cloves garlic, sliced
6 tablespoons olive oil
2 ounces anchovies
1 teaspoon red pepper flakes
½ cup capers, drained
2 cups tomatoes, chopped
1 pound uncooked linguine
½ cup toasted breadcrumbs
¼ cup chopped fresh parsley
¼ cup Parmesan cheese

Bring a large pot of water to a boil. While it is heating, add the garlic and 4 tablespoons of the olive oil to a large skillet. Cook the garlic over medium heat for 1 minute. Add the anchovies to the pan and cook until they melt into the olive oil. Add the red pepper flakes and capers and cook for about 1 minute. Add 2 cups of the boiling water to the skillet and cook for another minute. Add the tomatoes to the skillet and bring the sauce to a boil and then reduce the heat to a simmer. Add the pasta to the boiling water and cook until it is not quite done. Using tongs, carefully transfer the pasta to the skillet with the sauce. Add another cup of water to the skillet and increase the heat to medium-high. Cook for a couple more minutes until the sauce reduces. Add the remaining 2 tablespoons of olive oil and toss the pasta with tongs. Top with breadcrumbs, parsley, and cheese just before serving.

August 2011
Oklahoma Living

Mark's Favorite Upside-Down Pizza

1 pound ground beef
15 ounces spaghetti sauce
browned sausage (optional)
pepperoni (optional)
sliced mushrooms (optional)
sliced olives (optional)
minced garlic (optional)
chopped onion (optional)
chopped green bell peppers (optional)
2 cups shredded mozzarella cheese
2 eggs
1 cup milk
1 tablespoon olive oil or grapeseed oil
1 cup all-purpose flour
½ teaspoon salt
Parmesan cheese

Preheat the oven to 400°F. Brown the ground beef and drain excess grease. Stir in the spaghetti sauce. Pour into the bottom of a 9-by-13-inch baking dish. Add any of the optional ingredients. Sprinkle with the mozzarella cheese. In a bowl, beat the eggs and milk. Add the oil, flour, and salt. Pour over the mozzarella cheese. Top with Parmesan cheese. Bake for 30 minutes; let stand for 10 minutes and cut into pieces.

Sue Robinson
Glencoe, Okla.
Central Rural Electric Cooperative

Taco Pasta

1 pound ground beef
1 package taco seasoning
12-ounce package colored spiral pasta, cooked and drained
1 onion, chopped
1 green bell pepper, chopped
1 red bell pepper, chopped
1 small bottle taco sauce
½ bottle Western dressing
1 cup shredded cheese
crushed tortilla chips

Cook the ground beef with the taco seasoning and drain excess grease. Mix all ingredients and top with crushed chips just before serving.

Pat Sewell
Porum, Okla.

Favorite Meatloaf

1 ½ pounds ground beef
½ pound ground pork
¼ cup finely chopped onion
2 teaspoons salt
¼ teaspoon black pepper
¼ teaspoon sage
¼ teaspoon poultry seasoning
1 tablespoon Worcestershire sauce
2 eggs
1 cup tomato juice
4 slices bread

Preheat the oven to 350°F. Combine the ground beef and ground pork with the onion, salt, pepper, sage, poultry seasoning, and Worcestershire sauce. Beat the eggs and add tomato juice. Cube the bread and soak it in the egg mixture. Beat well. Add to the beef mixture and mix lightly. Pack into a 9-by-5-inch loaf pan and bake for 1 hour and 15 minutes. Let stand for 10 minutes, then drain off liquid and turn out of the pan. Spread with ketchup or hot tomato sauce.

January 1958
Oklahoma Rural News

Bacon-Cheeseburger Meatloaf

1 pound ground beef
10 slices bacon, cooked and crumbled
8-ounce package shredded sharp cheddar cheese
2 eggs, beaten
¼ cup toasted breadcrumbs
¼ cup mayonnaise
1 tablespoon Worcestershire sauce
¼ teaspoon salt
¼ teaspoon black pepper
⅓ cup ketchup
2 tablespoons mustard
3-ounce can French fried onions

Preheat the oven to 350°F. In a large bowl, combine the ground beef, bacon, cheese, eggs, breadcrumbs, mayonnaise, Worcestershire sauce, salt, and pepper, mixing well. In a small bowl, combine the ketchup and mustard; stir ¼ cup of the ketchup sauce into the meat mixture. Press meat mixture into a 9-by-5-inch loaf pan, or shape into a loaf and place on a broiler pan. Spread the remaining ketchup sauce over the top of the loaf. Bake for 40 minutes. Remove from the oven and top with French fried onions. Bake for another 10 to 15 minutes or until the meat is no longer pink.

John Long
Sand Springs, Okla.
Indian Electric Cooperative

A "**Helpful Hint**" from the November 1964 *Oklahoma Rural News*: In the summer months, cook meatloaf in muffin tins. It cooks much faster and everyone can be individually served.

Grandma's Meatballs

For the meatballs:
1 pound ground beef
2 eggs
crushed crackers
2 tablespoons water
salt and black pepper, to taste

For the sauce:
1 onion, chopped
2 tablespoons margarine
16-ounce can tomato sauce
16 ounces water
1 teaspoon granulated sugar
salt, to taste
½ teaspoon baking soda

Combine the meatball ingredients and brown in a skillet, adding just enough crackers to help the meat stick into balls. Form small balls no larger than 1 to 1 ½ inches in diameter. For the sauce, sauté the onion in margarine. Add the tomato sauce, water, sugar, and salt to taste. Bring to a boil and add the baking soda. Add the meatballs to the sauce and simmer for 1 hour. Serve with spaghetti.

Tory Tedder
Norman, Okla.
Oklahoma Electric Cooperative

Grandma's Meatballs

Hamburger Stuffed in French Bread

2 pounds ground beef
1 teaspoon salt
1 teaspoon black pepper
1 green bell pepper, diced
½ cup diced celery
1 can cheddar cheese soup
¼ cup milk
1 tablespoon Worcestershire sauce
1 loaf French bread, unsliced
2 cups breadcrumbs
3 slices cheese

Preheat the oven to 350°F. Brown the ground beef, drain excess grease, and add the salt, pepper, bell pepper, celery, soup, milk, and Worcestershire sauce; simmer for 5 minutes. Slice the top off the bread and hollow out the center. Shred the hollowed-out bread for the breadcrumbs. Mix the breadcrumbs into the meat. Place the mixture in the loaf of bread. Lay the cheese slices on top and cover with the top of the bread. Place on a baking sheet and bake for 8 minutes.

Mary Ann Koehn
Fairview, Okla.
Cimarron Electric Cooperative

BBQ Beef Brisket

4-to-5-pound beef brisket
1 tablespoon Worcestershire sauce
2 tablespoons liquid smoke
2 teaspoons salt
4 tablespoons soy sauce
2 teaspoons garlic powder
2 teaspoons onion salt
2 teaspoons black pepper
1 tablespoon celery seeds

For the brisket sauce:
3 tablespoons brown sugar
1 teaspoon dry mustard
3 to 4 drops hot sauce, such as Tabasco
½ cup ketchup
1 teaspoon lemon juice
1 tablespoon soy sauce
dash nutmeg

Preheat the oven to 300°F. Combine all brisket ingredients and marinate the brisket overnight or longer, turning several times to cover both sides well. Bake for 3 ½ hours or until cooked thoroughly; drain the liquid and discard. Combine all sauce ingredients and cover brisket completely before serving.

Neta Liebscher
El Reno, Okla.
Cimarron Electric Cooperative

Slow-cooked Cube Steak with Gravy

4 4-ounce cube steaks
salt and black pepper, to taste
¼ cup all-purpose flour
⅓ cup vegetable oil
1 teaspoon beef bouillon granules
1 onion, sliced into rings (optional)
mushrooms, sliced (optional)

Season the cube steaks on both sides with salt and pepper. Pour the flour onto a shallow plate and press the steaks into the flour; shake off excess flour. Heat the oil in a large skillet with a lid over medium-high heat. Place the steaks into the hot oil and cook, uncovered, until golden brown on both sides, about 3 minutes per side. Pour water into the skillet to almost cover the steaks. Stir the beef bouillon and salt to taste into the water. Bring to a boil; reduce the heat to medium-low, cover, and simmer until very tender, about 2 hours. If desired, add onion or mushrooms as it simmers.

Mary J. Moerbe
Blackwell, Okla.
Kay Electric Cooperative

Oklahoma Barbequed Spareribs

4 to 5 pounds spareribs in 2 pieces
salt and freshly ground black pepper

For the barbeque sauce:
½ cup honey
⅔ cup soy sauce
⅔ cup ketchup
1 teaspoon dry mustard
1 teaspoon paprika
½ teaspoon hot sauce, such as Tabasco
1 clove garlic, finely mashed
1 teaspoon salt

Salt and pepper the spareribs and brown them on a grill over moderate fire, turning them once or twice. Prepare a pan from a double thickness of heavy-duty aluminum foil to fit the spareribs by turning up the edges of the foil 1 ½ inches all around. Miter the corners so it will be secure. Combine all barbeque sauce ingredients in a small bowl. As soon as spareribs have browned, transfer them to the foil pan and spoon about 1 cup of the sauce over the meat. Place the pan on the center of the grill and continue cooking for about 1 ½ hours longer. Baste with the rest of the sauce.

August 1958
Oklahoma Rural News

Oklahoma Barbequed Spareribs

A "**Helpful Hint**" from the February 1953 *Oklahoma Rural News*: Use kitchen tongs instead of a fork when turning steak or chops in the broiler. This prevents piercing the surface of the meat, which allows the juices to escape.

Beef Kabobs

1 pound beef sirloin steak
¼ cup dry red wine
2 tablespoons minced onion
1 tablespoon lemon juice
1 tablespoon olive or salad oil
1 clove garlic, minced
1 teaspoon basil leaves
1 teaspoon granulated sugar
½ teaspoon salt
½ teaspoon thyme leaves
1 small green bell pepper, cut into 6 pieces
6 medium mushrooms

Trim fat from the outside of the steak; cut into 1-inch cubes. Combine all remaining ingredients, except mushrooms, in a zip-top bag. Place the beef cubes in the bag and turn to coat the meat completely. Let the bag marinate in the refrigerator for 6 to 8 hours or overnight. Pour off and reserve the marinade. Alternately thread the beef cubes, bell pepper, and mushrooms on skewers; brush with marinade. Place kabobs on a grill over coals (or on a rack in the broiler pan) so the meat is 3 to 4 inches from the heat. Broil for 15 to 20 minutes, depending on the level of doneness desired. Turn and brush with marinade occasionally.

August 1985
Oklahoma Rural News

Beef Kabobs

River's Bend Short Ribs

"My family and guests have always loved this recipe. The lemon juice helps to tenderize the ribs. The gravy is superb. I was raised on water gravy during the Depression years."

4 pounds beef short ribs
2 large onions, sliced
1 package onion soup mix
2 tablespoons lemon juice
12 ounces beer
½ cup water
salt, to taste
cornstarch

Preheat the oven to 325°F. Brown the ribs in hot fat; drain. Transfer them to a large baking pan. Arrange the onion slices between and over ribs. Sprinkle with the onion soup mix. Mix the lemon juice and beer and pour over the ribs. Bake for 1 ½ hours or until tender. Transfer the meat and onions to a serving platter. Skim excess fat from the meat juices. In a saucepan, combine the meat juices, water, and salt to taste. To thicken the broth, make a paste of cornstarch and water. Cook until it reaches the desired consistency and pour over the meat. Garnish with lemon slices and parsley.

Virginia Green
Beggs, Okla.
East Central Oklahoma Electric Cooperative

Uniquely Oklahoman

Watermelon Barbeque Sauce

½ cup watermelon juice
½ cup balsamic vinegar
¼ cup brown sugar
¼ cup soy sauce
2 tablespoons vegetable oil
2 tablespoons Dijon mustard
2 cloves garlic, minced
2 teaspoons red pepper flakes

Stir all ingredients together. Pour enough sauce over vegetables and chicken, pork, or shellfish to marinate. Cover and refrigerate for several hours or overnight. Baste main dish with additional watermelon sauce while grilling or broiling. If the sauce has not been used for marinating or basting, it can be spooned over cooked vegetables and meats.

August 2001
Oklahoma Living

Beef-Stuffed Tomatoes

1 pound ground beef
1 small onion, chopped
4 large tomatoes
1 medium zucchini, shredded and drained
½ cup shredded mozzarella cheese
¼ cup Parmesan cheese
¼ cup soft breadcrumbs
1 teaspoon garlic salt
½ teaspoon oregano leaves
⅛ teaspoon black pepper

Combine the ground beef and onion. Arrange in a ring in an all-plastic sieve or small colander. Place the sieve in a bowl and microwave on high for 2 minutes. Stir to break up the beef. Continue cooking on high for 2 minutes. Remove from the microwave and stir. Meanwhile, cut a ½-inch slice off the top of each tomato. Scoop out the tomato pulp, leaving a ¼-inch-thick shell. Combine the beef, zucchini, cheeses, breadcrumbs, garlic salt, oregano, and pepper. Divide the beef mixture into four portions. Place one portion into each tomato cup, rounding the top. Place the tomatoes in a circle on a microwave-safe plate. Microwave on high for 5 minutes, rotating them after 2 ½ minutes.

September 1983
Oklahoma Rural News

Beef-Stuffed Tomatoes

Uniquely Oklahoman

Carolee's Barbeque Brisket

3-to-4-pound beef brisket
liquid smoke
Worcestershire sauce
celery salt
onion powder
garlic powder

For the sauce:
¾ cup chopped onion
½ cup canola oil
¾ cup ketchup
¾ cup water
⅓ cup lemon juice
3 tablespoons granulated sugar
3 tablespoons Worcestershire sauce
2 tablespoons prepared mustard
1 teaspoon salt

Preheat the oven to 275°F. Sprinkle both sides of the brisket generously with liquid smoke, Worcestershire sauce, celery salt, onion powder, and garlic powder. Cover tightly with heavy-duty aluminum foil and let it marinate in the refrigerator for about 12 hours. Bake, covered, for 1 hour per pound of brisket. Chill thoroughly and slice thin. For the sauce, cook the onion in the oil until tender but not brown. Add the remaining ingredients and simmer for about 30 minutes. Pour the sauce on the brisket and reheat to serve.

Judith Whelchel
Blanchard, Okla.
Oklahoma Electric Cooperative

Ginger-Honey Pork Tenderloin

1 tablespoon freshly grated ginger
3 tablespoons honey
1 tablespoon lemon juice
1 tablespoon soy sauce
1 pound pork tenderloin
½ teaspoon salt
¼ teaspoon black pepper

Whisk together the ginger, honey, lemon juice, and soy sauce. Sprinkle the pork tenderloin with salt and pepper. Grill the pork, basting with the sauce, until cooked through.

Sierra D. Jones
Moore, Okla.
Oklahoma Electric Cooperative

Baked Pork Chops

6 to 8 bone-in pork chops
¼ cup water
1 can mushroom soup
1 package brown gravy, such as Pioneer, prepared
grated Parmesan cheese

Preheat the oven to 375°F. Place the pork chops in a greased baking dish. Add the water and cover with aluminum foil. Place in the oven and bake for 1 hour. Remove from the oven and place the chops on the aluminum foil. Pour off the fat and scrape the dish. Sprinkle the chops liberally with grated Parmesan cheese. Turn the chops over and place them back into the dish. Spoon the soup and prepared gravy over the chops. Sprinkle Parmesan cheese liberally over the gravy-covered chops. Place back into the oven until the cheese browns lightly.

Ronald O. Mannbeck
Owasso, Okla.
Verdigris Valley Electric Cooperative

Lemon Chicken

4 boneless, skinless chicken breasts
1 teaspoon salt
½ teaspoon black pepper
½ cup all-purpose flour
4 tablespoons butter
2 tablespoons olive oil
¼ cup chicken broth
¼ cup lemon juice
8 lemon slices
¼ cup chopped fresh flat-leaf parsley
lemon slices for garnish

Cut each breast in half lengthwise. Place the chicken between two sheets of heavy-duty plastic wrap; pound each breast to ¼-inch thickness with a rolling pin or the flat side of a meat mallet. Sprinkle each breast with salt and pepper. Lightly dredge the chicken in flour, shaking off excess flour. In a large nonstick skillet over medium-high heat, heat 1 tablespoon of the butter with 1 tablespoon of the oil. Cook half of the chicken for 2 to 3 minutes on each side or until golden brown and cooked through. Transfer the chicken to a serving platter and keep warm. Repeat procedure with 1 tablespoon of the butter and the remaining oil and chicken. Add the chicken broth and lemon juice to the skillet and cook for 1 to 2 minutes or until sauce is slightly thickened, stirring to loosen particles from bottom of the skillet. Add the lemon slices. Remove the skillet from the heat. Add the parsley and remaining 2 tablespoons of butter, and stir until the butter melts. Pour the sauce over the chicken. Garnish with additional lemon slices and serve immediately.

Eloise Ragsdale
Custer City, Okla.
Kiwash Electric Cooperative

Artichoke Chicken and Olives

1 ½ pounds skinless, boneless chicken breast halves
2 cups sliced fresh mushrooms
14 ½-ounce can diced tomatoes, undrained
8-to-9-ounce package frozen artichoke hearts
1 cup chicken broth
1 medium onion, chopped
½ cup sliced ripe olives or ¼ cup capers, drained
¼ cup dry white wine or chicken broth
3 tablespoons quick-cooking tapioca
2 to 3 teaspoons curry powder
¾ teaspoon dried thyme, crushed
¼ teaspoon salt
¼ teaspoon black pepper

Rinse chicken; set aside. In a 3 ½-quart or 4-quart slow cooker, combine the mushrooms, tomatoes, artichoke hearts, broth, onion, olives or capers, and wine or broth. Stir in the tapioca, curry powder, thyme, salt, and pepper. Add the chicken and spoon some of the mixture over the chicken. Cover; cook on low for 7 to 8 hours or on high for 3 ½ to 4 hours. Serve over hot couscous.

Michelle Lawson
Perry, Okla.
Central Rural Electric Cooperative

PUT NON-LAYERS IN THE FREEZER, SAVE GRAIN, AND PROVIDE GOOD WINTER EATING

With an up-and-coming flock of pullets to take over the main laying duties of the hen-house, the wise homemaker will cull the old hens which are not earning their keep. Kill them and store them in the family freezer or food locker. You will save valuable grain and at the same time, tuck away many delicious meals for wintertime dining pleasure.

Freezing chicken is not a difficult task. To save freezer space, cook the bony pieces (wings, necks and back) and freeze creamed chicken or chicken à la king. Freeze the meaty pieces separately to be used for stew or fricassee when needed.

Oklahoma Rural News
October 1948

Herbed Chicken

1 to 2 tablespoons olive oil
seasoned salt
6 boneless, skinless chicken thighs
2 to 3 cloves garlic, finely chopped
1 cup chicken broth or water
3 to 4 sprigs fresh thyme, chopped
2 bay leaves
2 tablespoons cornstarch
¼ cup cold water

Heat the oil in a heavy skillet. Sprinkle seasoned salt on the chicken thighs and place the chicken in the hot skillet. Brown the chicken and add chopped garlic. Deglaze the pan with chicken broth and scrape the pan to remove any particles. Add thyme and bay leaves to the chicken and broth. Reduce the heat and cover. Cook until the chicken is very tender, at least 45 minutes. Before serving, increase heat. Mix cornstarch in cold water and stir in slowly, stirring constantly until bubbly and thickened. Serve over rice cooked in chicken broth with garlic and thyme.

Lisa Davis
Tulsa, Okla.

Teriyaki Chicken

Teriyaki Chicken

¾ cup teriyaki sauce
1 teaspoon ground ginger
1 teaspoon garlic powder
4 pounds frying chicken pieces (breasts, thighs, and legs)
1 egg, beaten
1½ cups finely minced pecans
1 cup all-purpose flour

Preheat the oven to 350°F. Combine teriyaki sauce, ginger, and garlic powder. Pour into a large zip-top bag and place the chicken pieces inside. Press air out, close securely, and turn over several times to coat the chicken completely. Refrigerate for 8 hours or overnight. Remove chicken, reserving marinade. Combine the egg and 2 tablespoons of reserved marinade; set aside. Combine the pecans and flour on large plate. Dip chicken pieces into egg mixture, then roll in pecan mixture, coating all sides. Place chicken pieces, skin side up, on a rack placed in a large baking pan. Bake for 50 minutes or until chicken is tender.

January 1985
Oklahoma Rural News

Uniquely Oklahoman

Cornmeal Oven-fried Chicken

½ cup cornmeal
½ cup dry breadcrumbs
2 tablespoons plus 2 teaspoons Parmesan cheese
2 tablespoons plus 2 teaspoons powdered American cheese (from macaroni and cheese box)
1 tablespoon dry parsley
1 tablespoon garlic salt
½ teaspoon black pepper
1 teaspoon onion powder
2 tablespoons Cajun seasoning
3 pounds chicken breasts, cut into pieces
1 to 2 tablespoons butter, melted

Preheat the oven to 350°F. In a large bowl, mix all ingredients, except chicken and butter. Dredge the chicken pieces in the cornmeal mixture and place the pieces in a 9-by-13-inch baking pan. Cover with foil and bake for 30 minutes. Remove the foil and drizzle with the butter. Return the dish to the oven, uncovered, and bake until the chicken juices run clear.

Annavee Kirby-Denny
Colcord, Okla.
Northeast Oklahoma Electric Cooperative

Crescent Chicken Squares

3 ounces cream cheese, softened
3 tablespoons butter, melted
3 cups cooked, cubed chicken
¼ teaspoon salt
⅛ teaspoon black pepper
2 tablespoons chopped chives
1 tablespoon chopped pimiento (optional)
1 can cream of chicken soup
2 8-ounce tubes crescent rolls
¾ cup seasoned crouton crumbs, finely ground

Preheat the oven to 350°F. Blend the cream cheese and 2 tablespoons of the butter until smooth. Add the chicken, salt, pepper, chives, pimiento, and soup; mix well. Separate crescent rolls into 4 rectangles per can and pinch the perforations firmly to seal. Spoon approximately ¾ cup of the chicken mixture onto the center of each rectangle. Gather the corners of the rectangle together and twist to seal in the chicken mixture. Brush the tops with the remaining tablespoon of butter and sprinkle with crouton crumbs. Place on an ungreased baking sheet and bake for 20 to 25 minutes.

Clara Schrader
Oklahoma City, Okla.
Oklahoma Electric Cooperative

Honey BBQ Chicken

½ cup brown sugar
3 tablespoons chili powder
¾ teaspoon black pepper
1 teaspoon salt
4 chicken breasts
¾ cup mustard
¾ cup white wine vinegar
6 tablespoons honey

In a zip-top bag, combine the brown sugar, chili powder, pepper, and salt. Add the chicken breasts to the bag and coat well. Refrigerate for 2 hours or overnight. In a medium bowl, whisk together the mustard, vinegar, and honey. Remove ½ cup of the mixture and set aside. Heat the grill to medium-low. Grill the chicken, covered, for 30 to 40 minutes, turning occasionally. Baste with the mustard sauce for the last 5 to 10 minutes. Serve with the reserved sauce.

LaDale Hymer
Cleveland, Okla.
Indian Electric Cooperative

Lila Clay's Chicken and Rice

½ cup butter
1 medium onion
6 chicken tenders
2 cans chicken broth
2 cups uncooked white rice
1 can carrots, drained (optional) or 1 can green peas, drained (optional)

Melt the butter over medium heat in a Dutch oven or heavy pot. Add the chopped onion. Place chicken tenders on top of the onion. Cook one side for about 2 minutes; turn and cook for 2 minutes on the other side. Remove the chicken. Add chicken broth and rice to the pot. Cut the chicken into bite-size pieces and return to the pot; cook until the rice is done. Turn the heat off and add carrots or peas if desired.

Linda Anderson
Wilburton, Okla.

Odie Bob's Chicken and Rice

1 whole chicken
1 whole onion, roughly chopped
1 tablespoon minced garlic
1 tablespoon salt
2 teaspoons black pepper
2 tablespoons Italian seasoning
2 bay leaves
2 pounds uncooked long-grain rice

Place the chicken in a large pot. Add the onion, garlic, salt, pepper, and Italian seasoning. Cover the chicken with water; boil until the chicken is fully cooked. Remove the chicken and shred the meat. Reserve 10 cups of the broth. Add the shredded chicken and the rice to the broth. Cover the pot. Bring the liquid to a boil and reduce the heat to a simmer. Cook until the rice is tender, adding additional liquid if necessary.

Odus Hennessee
Medicine Park, Okla.
Cotton Electric Cooperative

A "**Helpful Hint**" from the February 1953 *Oklahoma Rural News*: A tablespoon of vinegar added to the water in which fish is simmered will make the fish firmer and whiter for serving.

Baked Salmon with Shrimp in a White Wine Cream Sauce

1 dozen shrimp, unpeeled
3 tablespoons butter
4 6-ounce salmon fillets
salt and black pepper
¼ cup water
4 large shallots, sliced
1 cup dry white wine or ½ cup lemon juice
1 pint heavy cream
2 sprigs thyme

Preheat the oven to 400°F. Peel the shrimp and set the shells aside. Devein the shrimp. Brush a baking dish with 1 tablespoon of the butter and place the salmon fillets in the dish. Sprinkle the salmon with salt and pepper and add the water. Bake for 10 to 14 minutes. Meanwhile, heat 1 tablespoon of the butter in a small saucepan. When the butter changes color, add the shallots and shrimp shells and cook for 10 minutes over medium heat. Add wine or lemon juice. Reduce the sauce by half and add the cream, thyme, and pepper to taste. Simmer for another 10 minutes. Strain the sauce to remove the shells and thyme. Heat the remaining tablespoon of butter in a small sauté pan. When the butter changes color, add the shrimp and cook for 5 minutes. Season with salt and pepper. Pour the sauce over the shrimp and salmon before serving.

Alain Buthion
Oklahoma City, Okla.

Fish Fillets over Zesty Lemon Rice

¼ cup butter or margarine
1 lemon, zested and juiced (about 3 tablespoons juice)
2 chicken bouillon cubes
½ teaspoon black pepper
1 cup cooked rice
10-ounce package frozen chopped broccoli, thawed and cooked until almost tender
1 cup shredded sharp cheddar cheese
1 pound fish fillets
½ teaspoon paprika

Preheat the oven to 375°F. Spray a 2-quart-square baking dish with nonstick cooking spray. Melt the butter in a small saucepan over medium heat. Add the lemon juice, bouillon cubes, and pepper; cook and stir for 2 minutes or until bouillon dissolves. Combine the rice, drained broccoli, cheese, and ¼ cup of the lemon sauce in a medium bowl; spread on the bottom of the prepared dish. Place fillets over the rice mixture. Pour remaining lemon sauce over the fillets. Sprinkle with lemon zest to taste. Bake, uncovered, for 20 minutes or until fish flakes easily when tested with a fork. Sprinkle evenly with paprika.

Sheryl Hanson
Morris, Okla.
East Central Oklahoma Electric Cooperative

Uniquely Oklahoman

Classic Fried Catfish

¾ cup yellow cornmeal
¼ cup all-purpose flour
2 teaspoons salt
1 teaspoon cayenne pepper
¼ teaspoon garlic powder
4 farm-raised catfish fillets
vegetable oil for frying

Combine the cornmeal, flour, salt, cayenne pepper, and garlic powder. Coat the catfish fillets with the mixture, shaking off the excess. Fill a deep pot or 12-inch skillet half full with vegetable oil. Heat the oil to 350°F. Add the catfish in a single layer and fry until golden brown, about 5 to 6 minutes. Remove and drain on paper towels.

September 1990
Oklahoma Rural News

Jambalaya

2 tablespoons bacon fat
1 tablespoon all-purpose flour
½ pound ham, cubed
1 large green bell pepper, chopped
2 cups cooked shrimp
2 ½ cups tomatoes
1 ½ cups water
1 large onion, chopped
1 clove garlic, chopped
1 tablespoon parsley, chopped
¾ cup uncooked rice

Preheat an electric skillet to 350°F. Melt the bacon fat. Stir in the flour. Add the ham and bell pepper. Cook, stirring, for about 5 minutes. Add the cooked shrimp, tomatoes, water, onion, garlic, and parsley. Bring to a boil and add the uncooked rice. Reduce the temperature to 225°F. Simmer for 30 minutes.

September 1958
Oklahoma Rural News

Sausage and Ham Jambalaya

8 ounces smoked sausage
8 ounces ham, diced
2 cans Cajun-style stewed tomatoes
1 can water
1 cup uncooked rice
1 large clove garlic, minced
1 medium onion, chopped
1 tablespoon chopped parsley
1 bay leaf

Brown the sausage and ham in a Dutch oven or large skillet. Add the tomatoes, water, rice, garlic, onion, parsley, and bay leaf. Cook uncovered for 20 minutes, stirring occasionally. Cover and simmer for 45 minutes, stirring occasionally. Remove the bay leaf before serving.

Jonna Hensley
Mooreland, Okla.
Northwestern Electric Cooperative

ELECTRIC AUTOMATIC FRY PAN HAS MANY USES IN TODAY'S KITCHEN

One of the most versatile of kitchen appliances is the electric automatic fry pan. It functions wonderfully in preparing bacon and eggs and all the other "standard" frying pan recipes, but it's not merely a skillet.

The automatic fry pan can perform many other kitchen tasks, from bun-warming to corn-popping. And its versatility makes it an inexpensive appliance to own.

The fry pan solves the case of the "jumping hostess," too. Several meals can be prepared by the homemaker right at the table, eliminating those annoying back-and-forth trips to and from a food preparation center away from the table.

Oklahoma Rural News
September 1958

This 1950s Jambalaya recipe (see page 124) can be cooked entirely in an electric skillet.

Corn and Wild Onions

7 slices bacon
½ cup chopped wild onions
4 eggs
1 can cream-style corn

Cut the bacon in small pieces and fry until crisp. Remove the bacon pieces and cook the wild onions in the bacon fat. Add the eggs and stir until cooked. Add the bacon and corn and heat until hot.

August 1995
Oklahoma Living

Sausage and Rice Casserole

1 pound sausage
3 cups water
½ cup chopped onion
½ cup chopped green bell pepper
4 stalks celery, chopped
1 cup uncooked long grain rice
1 small package slivered almonds
1 package chicken noodle soup mix, such as Lipton

Preheat the oven to 375°F. Brown the sausage and drain. Add the water, onion, bell pepper, and celery and bring to a boil. Add the rice, almonds, and soup mix. Simmer for 30 minutes. Transfer to a baking dish, sprinkle breadcrumbs on top, and bake until the crumbs are browned.

Nancy J. Martin
Oklahoma City, Okla.
Oklahoma Electric Cooperative

Company Casserole

8-ounce package medium noodles
1 ½ pounds ground beef
2 tablespoons margarine
1 teaspoon salt
black pepper
¼ teaspoon garlic salt
8-ounce can tomato sauce
1 cup creamed cottage cheese
1 cup sour cream
6 green onions, chopped
¾ cup shredded sharp cheddar cheese

Preheat the oven to 350°F. Cook the noodles in salted boiling water until tender; drain and rinse. In a skillet, cook the ground beef in the margarine until it is no longer pink. Add the salt, pepper, garlic salt, and tomato sauce and simmer for 5 minutes. In a bowl, combine the cottage cheese, sour cream, green onion, and noodles. Create alternating layers of the noodle mixture and meat sauce in a shallow 2-quart baking dish. Top with shredded cheese. Bake for 30 minutes.

Kathy Kaad
Porter, Okla.
Lake Region Electric Cooperative

Wild Onions and Eggs

"Gathering wild onions in spring is a ritual among the Oklahoma Cherokee, as well as the other tribes who live where these wonderful plants grow. In the early spring, many Indian churches, stomp grounds, clubs, and other groups hold wild onion dinners. Families and friends also often make an outing of gathering wild onions and eating them together. The location of one's wild onion patch is often a closely guarded secret! Today freshly picked wild onions are often frozen and kept for months so they can be enjoyed throughout the year."

2 to 3 tablespoons bacon drippings
1 cup chopped wild onions
¼ cup water
6 to 7 eggs, beaten

Warm the bacon drippings in a skillet over medium heat. Add the chopped onions and the water. Simmer, while stirring, until the onions are tender. Add additional water if needed. When the onions are tender, and most of the water has cooked away, add the eggs and scramble.

The Cherokee Nation

Turkey Gravy

4 cups turkey broth
¼ cup fat drippings
¼ cup cornstarch
1 cooked turkey liver, chopped
½ teaspoon salt
¼ teaspoon thyme
⅛ teaspoon black pepper

Bring the broth to a boil. In a separate pan, add ¼ cup of fat drippings reserved from a turkey roaster along with the cornstarch. Cook over medium heat, stirring constantly, for about 5 minutes or until browned. Gradually add the broth and bring to a boil, stirring constantly, until the gravy thickens. Add the liver, salt, thyme, and pepper. Simmer for a few minutes.

October 1974
Oklahoma Rural News

A "**Helpful Hint**" from the February 1953 *Oklahoma Rural News*: When gravy is too salty, add a sprinkle of brown sugar. Does not sweeten the gravy or spoil the flavor in any way.

Mexi-Chili Casserole

1 pound ground beef
1 can kidney beans, drained
15-ounce can mild enchilada sauce
8-ounce can tomato sauce
1 small onion, diced
6-ounce package corn chips
2 cups shredded cheddar cheese
1 ½ cups sour cream

Preheat the oven to 375°F. In a skillet, brown the ground beef. Combine the beans, enchilada sauce, tomato sauce, and onion in a medium bowl. Set aside 1 cup of corn chips and ½ cup of the cheese. Add the remaining corn chips, cheese, and meat to the beans; stir. Pour the mixture into a 2-quart baking dish and bake for 20 to 25 minutes, until heated through. Spread the sour cream on top and sprinkle with the reserved cheese. Arrange the remaining corn chips around the edge. Return the casserole to the oven for 3 to 4 minutes or until cheese is melted.

April 1982
Oklahoma Rural News

Pseudo-Enchiladas

1 medium onion, diced
2 tablespoons olive oil
2 pounds ground beef
2 4-ounce cans diced green chilies
1 package taco seasoning
8 burrito-size flour tortillas
2 cups shredded taco-blend cheese
28-ounce can red enchilada sauce

Preheat the oven to 350°F. In a large skillet, sauté the onion in the oil over medium-low heat until tender. Transfer the onion to a small bowl. Add the ground beef to the skillet. Brown and drain the ground beef. Mix in the onion, chilies, and taco seasoning. Spoon an eighth of the meat mixture into each tortilla and sprinkle cheese on top of each. Reserve ½ cup of the shredded cheese for the topping. Roll up the filled tortillas and place them in a 9-by-13-inch baking dish. Pour the enchilada sauce over the tortillas, separating them so the sauce runs down between the tortillas. Sprinkle the remaining cheese over the top. Cover the dish with foil and bake for 30 to 35 minutes.

Mikel Araujo
Duncan, Okla.

Betty Moe's Mexican Chicken Casserole

- 1 bag toasted corn chips, such as Doritos
- 1 cooked whole chicken, deboned and shredded or 4 12 ½-ounce cans chicken breast
- 1 can cream of celery soup
- 1 can cream of mushroom soup
- 1 can diced tomatoes and green chilies, such as Rotel
- 1 onion, finely chopped
- ½ green bell pepper, finely chopped
- 2 cups shredded fiesta-blend cheese
- 1 ½ cups chicken broth

Preheat the oven to 350°F. Layer the bottom of a 9-by-13-inch baking dish with corn chips; add a layer of shredded chicken. In medium bowl, combine the soups and diced tomatoes and green chilies. Spoon the mixture over the chicken. Add a layer of onion and bell pepper and spread the cheese on top. Pour the broth over the entire casserole. Bake for 1 hour. Remove and let stand for 15 minutes before serving.

Sheila Anderson
Lawton, Okla.

SPICY CASSEROLE QUICK WAY TO FEED YOUR FAMILY

If, like most busy homemakers, you rely on convenience foods to help you fix quickie meals, you'll want to add this casserole to your recipe collection. It's made with foods that give a flavor that youngsters and grownups, alike, enjoy eating: ground beef, kidney beans, tomato sauce, corn chips, cheddar cheese and sour cream. This winning combination saves you time and money.

Best of all, this tasty Mexi-Chili Casserole (see page 128) uses convenience foods to cut down on preparation. You don't need to spend hours compounding a spicy sauce and waiting while it cooks to perfection. Just open a can of mildly seasoned enchilada sauce and blend with tomato sauce and onion to give your recipe zest. You can even use instant minced onion to save time and tears. Cheese goes into the mixture, too, and it bakes in a jiffy. Corn chips provide crunch and give the flavor of tamale pie without the effort.

The topping of dairy sour cream, a handful of shredded cheddar cheese and a circle of corn chips goes on after baking the casserole 20 to 25 minutes. After the final trip to the oven to melt the cheese, it's ready to serve. Serve Mexi-Chili Casserole with tossed green salad, crusty hard rolls and butter. Milk is the beverage to balance the meal and give cool contrast to your hot 'n hearty casserole.

Oklahoma Rural News
April 1982

Western Casserole

1 pound ground beef
2 tablespoons oil
½ cup chopped onion
1 cup chopped celery
¼ cup chopped green bell pepper
1 cup uncooked rice
2 ½ cups tomatoes
1 cup water
2 teaspoons salt
2 to 3 teaspoons chili powder
¼ teaspoon black pepper
½ tablespoon Worcestershire sauce

Preheat the oven to 325°F. In a large skillet, brown the ground beef in oil; remove the beef and set aside. Sauté the onion, celery, bell pepper, and rice in the beef drippings until brown. Stir in the tomatoes, water, salt, chili powder, black pepper, Worcestershire sauce, and beef. Bring to a boil. Transfer to a baking dish and bake for 45 minutes. Top with cheese, if desired.

Cheryl Hyde
Lexington, Okla.
Oklahoma Electric Cooperative

Cheesy Chili Mac

2 tablespoons butter
1 cup chopped onion
¾ cup chopped green bell pepper
2 15 ½-ounce cans dark red kidney beans, drained
16-ounce can tomatoes, undrained
8-ounce can tomato sauce
1 tablespoon chili powder
1 teaspoon Worcestershire sauce
hot pepper sauce
2 cups shredded cheddar cheese
2 cups cooked elbow macaroni

Melt the butter in a 4-quart Dutch oven or large pot. Sauté the onion and bell pepper until tender, about 5 minutes. Stir in the beans, tomatoes, tomato sauce, chili powder, Worcestershire sauce, and hot pepper sauce. Bring to a boil, stirring frequently; reduce the heat. Simmer, covered, for 30 minutes, stirring occasionally. Remove from heat. Stir in the cheese until melted. If necessary, return to low heat to finish melting cheese, but do not boil. Stir in the macaroni. Heat to serving temperature and serve immediately.

October 1982
Oklahoma Rural News

Cheesy Chili Mac

Tanshpashofa

- 1 ½ to 2 ½ cups dry cracked ('pashofa) corn
- water
- 1 to 3 pounds pork loin roast
- salt and black pepper, to taste
- 3 tablespoons vegetable oil

Pick through the dry cracked corn to remove any soybeans, debris, or yellow kernels. Rinse off any powder and floating hulls in a strainer or a saucepan with cold water. Soak the corn in cold water for at least 4 hours, rinsing every 2 hours or as often as possible. Rinse once more and add water 3 times the volume of the corn. (Do not add salt to the corn at this point, as that makes it stick to the pan.) Cover the pot and bring the corn to a boil. Reduce the heat to a simmer and vent the lid to allow steam to escape for the first 15 minutes. Simmer the corn for at least 8 hours, stirring every 2 hours to keep it from sticking. After the corn has simmered for about 2 hours, start the pork. Allow the pork to come to room temperature. Cut palm-size meat portions away from the bone; reserve the bones. Salt and pepper the meat. Heat a large skillet over high heat and add the oil. Place the bones in the center of the skillet with the pork slices around it. Brown all sides of the pork over high heat. Reduce the heat to medium, cover, and cook until the juices are no longer red. Place the browned pork and bones in a slow cooker or a large cooking pot. Deglaze the skillet with 2 cups of water. Pour that water over the pork and add enough additional water so that the pork is almost covered. Place a lid on the slow cooker or pot and simmer for at least 6 hours, until the pork is falling apart. Remove the bones with tongs. At least 2 hours before serving, add the cooked corn to the slow cooker or cooking pot and simmer, stirring occasionally. Serve with fry bread and salt pork on the side.

Pamela Filipelli
Sulphur, Okla.
People's Electric Cooperative

Ham and Mushroom Casserole

- 3 cups uncooked noodles
- 4 cups béchamel sauce
- ¼ pound American cheese, diced
- ¾ teaspoon onion powder or 1 tablespoon grated onion
- 4 stalks celery, sliced
- 6-ounce can mushrooms
- 3 cups diced ham
- buttered breadcrumbs

Preheat the oven to 375°F. Cook the noodles in boiling, slightly salted water; drain. Heat the béchamel sauce and melt the cheese into the heated sauce. Brown the onion, celery, and mushrooms in hot fat and add to the cheese sauce. Combine the cheese sauce with the noodles and ham and transfer to a greased baking dish. Cover with buttered breadcrumbs and bake for 30 minutes or until the crumbs are browned.

March 1948
Oklahoma Rural News

Around the World

Coconut-Orange Chicken Fajitas
(see page 135).

Huevos Rancheros

"Travelers in Mexico may enjoy an eye-opener of coffee and rolls, but this 'first breakfast' is often followed by a heartier 'second breakfast.' To sustain tourists for long hours of sightseeing the second breakfast may feature Huevos Rancheros. These Mexican country-style eggs are served fried on tortillas with a well-flavored tomato sauce. A substantial offering, it can come to brunch or lunch as a great change-of-pace dish."

2 tablespoons butter
½ cup finely chopped onion
½ cup finely chopped green bell pepper
1 clove garlic, minced
28-ounce can plum tomatoes, drained and chopped
½ teaspoon salt
½ teaspoon cilantro or dried parsley
⅛ teaspoon black pepper
6 6-inch soft corn tortillas
6 eggs
butter
1 cup shredded cheddar cheese
avocado slices (optional)

Melt the butter. Sauté onion, bell pepper, and garlic until tender but not browned. Add the tomatoes, salt, cilantro or parsley, and pepper. Simmer, uncovered, for 15 minutes or until sauce is thickened. Lightly brown the tortillas on both sides in a small amount of butter in a skillet until heated through and softened, but not crisp. Keep warm on an oven-safe platter covered with foil. (Don't hold longer than it takes to fry the eggs, or the tortillas will toughen.) Fry the eggs in butter, sunny side up. Place an egg in the center of each tortilla; surround with tomato sauce mixture. Sprinkle with cheese. Garnish with avocado if desired.

November 1984
Oklahoma Rural News

Huevos Rancheros

Mexican Brunch Chocolate

1 ½ quarts chocolate milk
1 teaspoon rum extract or ½ teaspoon angostura bitters

Heat milk to serving temperature. Remove from heat. Stir in extract or bitters. Whip until frothy and serve.

November 1984
Oklahoma Rural News

Tamale Pie

"Some of the best dishes of the Southwest borrow heavily from the finest Spanish and Mexican cooking. A typical dish is a Tamale Pie. Tamale Pie is great for a crowd. Prepare it ahead of time and keep it in the refrigerator until an hour before serving time. Then set it in a moderate oven to bake while you wait for the crowd to assemble. Your friends will savor the combination of the cornmeal crust and its spicy ground beef filling."

⅔ cup yellow cornmeal
1 ½ teaspoons salt
2 cups boiling water
2 tablespoons margarine
1 small onion, chopped
½ pound ground beef
1 small can tomato paste
¼ cup sliced stuffed olives
½ cup sliced ripe olives
½ green bell pepper, diced
1 teaspoon chili powder
¼ cup beef bouillon or consommé
½ can whole kernel corn
dash cayenne pepper
½ cup shredded cheese
paprika

Preheat the oven to 350°F. Stir the cornmeal and ½ teaspoon of the salt into rapidly boiling water. Cook and stir until thick. Remove from heat. In a heavy skillet, melt the margarine and brown the onion in it. Add the ground beef. Stir and cook until the meat is no longer pink. Add the tomato paste, olives, bell pepper, chili powder, bouillon or consommé, corn, cayenne pepper, and the remaining teaspoon of salt. Stir well. Taste to be sure there is enough salt. Line a shallow baking dish with part of the cornmeal mixture. Pour the meat and vegetable mixture into the dish. Drop remaining the cornmeal mixture by the spoonful on top of the meat; sprinkle shredded cheese over the top. Sprinkle paprika liberally over the surface. Bake for 1 hour.

January 1954
Oklahoma Rural News

Coconut-Orange Chicken Fajitas

4 boneless, skinless chicken breasts
1 cup orange juice
2 tablespoons lime juice
1 teaspoon garlic powder
2 teaspoons light soy sauce
1 teaspoon salt
4 tablespoons coconut oil
1 red bell pepper, seeded and sliced lengthwise
cheddar cheese
sour cream
flour tortillas

Dice the chicken breasts into 1-inch cubes. Place the chicken into a gallon-size zip-top bag with the orange juice, lime juice, garlic powder, soy sauce, and salt. Place the bag in the refrigerator and marinate the chicken for at least 4 hours. Drain the chicken and discard the marinade. In a skillet, melt 2 tablespoons of the coconut oil over medium-high heat. When water droplets sizzle in the oil, add half of the chicken. Fry for roughly 3 minutes before turning it and frying for 3 more minutes on the other side. Adjust the heat if necessary. Transfer the chicken to a serving dish and pour the juices from the skillet over it. Cook the remaining chicken in the remaining oil. Remove the chicken with a slotted spoon, and sauté the red bell pepper in the skillet juices until crisp-tender. Serve with sour cream and shredded cheddar in tortillas.

Ariel Keith
Noble, Okla.
Oklahoma Electric Cooperative

Chicken Tostadas

6-ounce can tomato paste
1½ cups water
1 package taco seasoning
4 cups cooked, chopped chicken
vegetable oil
12 flour tortillas
1 can refried beans, heated
½ medium head iceberg lettuce, shredded
3 cups shredded cheddar cheese
2 ripe avocados, cut into thin wedges
2 tomatoes, chopped
sour cream

In a saucepan, combine the tomato paste, water, and taco seasoning; whisk until smooth. Add chicken; heat through. Meanwhile, heat ¾ inch of the vegetable oil to 375°F in a 10-inch skillet. Fry the tortillas in the oil one at a time, until crisp and puffed. After frying, place the tortillas on paper towels to drain and cover to keep them warm. To assemble the tostadas, spread each tortilla with warm beans. Top with equal portions of chicken mixture, lettuce, and cheese. Garnish with avocado slices, tomatoes, and sour cream. Serve with salsa or taco sauce if desired.

March 1980
Oklahoma Rural News

Jo's Beef Empanadas

1 cup all-purpose flour
½ teaspoon baking powder
½ teaspoon salt
¼ cup shortening
2 ¼ cups plus 1 tablespoon cold water
1 pound beef stew meat
1 tablespoon meat seasoning
1 ½ tablespoons steak sauce, such as A-1
salt and black pepper, to taste
2 jalapeños, seeded and diced
1 onion, diced
1 tomato, diced
4 cups shredded cheese
1 egg

Preheat the oven to 375°F. Mix the flour, baking powder, and salt in a medium bowl. Cut in the shortening with a pastry blender or two knives until the mixture resembles coarse crumbs. Gradually add ¼ cup of the water and stir until the mixture forms into a ball. Knead the dough on a lightly floured surface for 5 minutes or until smooth and elastic. Wrap tightly in plastic wrap; refrigerate. In a medium bowl, combine the beef, seasoning, steak sauce, salt, and pepper. Mix until the meat is thoroughly coated. To a stew pot over medium heat, add the meat mixture and 2 cups of water. Cook until the meat can be easily shredded, about 3 hours. Shred the meat and add the jalapeños, onion, and tomato. Cook for another 15 minutes. Turn off the heat and let the meat mixture cool. Divide the dough into six pieces. Roll out each piece on a lightly floured surface into a 7-inch round; place the dough rounds on a greased or parchment-lined baking sheet. Spoon the meat filling and cheese onto half of the dough rounds. Beat the egg and remaining tablespoon of water; brush onto the edges of the dough rounds. Fold the dough rounds in half to enclose the filling. Press the tops lightly to remove excess air. Seal the edges with a fork. Brush the empanadas with the remaining egg wash. Bake for 18 to 20 minutes or until golden brown.

Joanne Shephard
Mustang, Okla.
Caddo Electric Cooperative

Brazilian Stroganoff

1 pound beef or chicken, cubed
2 tablespoons butter
1 onion, chopped
1 clove garlic, minced
1 teaspoon salt
1 pound champignon mushrooms
2 tablespoons ketchup
1 tablespoon mustard
1 teaspoon Worcestershire sauce
½ cup heavy cream
potato sticks

In a large saucepan over medium heat, sauté the beef or chicken in the butter with the onion, garlic, and salt. Add the mushrooms. Cook for 5 minutes; check meat for doneness. Add the ketchup, mustard, Worcestershire sauce, and cream. Mix briefly. Serve over rice and top with potato sticks.

Nanda Thompson
Broken Arrow, Okla.

Slow Cooker Carnitas

3 pounds pork shoulder
1 orange, juiced
1 onion, quartered
4 cloves garlic, peeled and halved
1 cinnamon stick
2 bay leaves
2 teaspoons kosher salt
corn or flour tortillas

Chop the pork into 2-inch pieces, trimming excess fat. Place the pork in a slow cooker, along with the juice of the orange and the onion, garlic, cinnamon stick, bay leaves, and salt. Cook on low for 8 to 10 hours. Use a slotted spoon to transfer the pork to a roasting pan, discarding the onion, cinnamon stick, and bay leaves. Bake for 20 minutes at 400°F to brown the meat. Shred the meat with a fork after removing from the oven. Serve the meat in tortillas with toppings such as red onion, cilantro, avocado, radish, queso fresco, and a side of lime wedges.

March 2012
Oklahoma Living

Slow Cooker Carnitas

Mexican Cornbread

16-ounce can cream-style corn
1 cup yellow cornmeal
½ teaspoon baking soda
1 teaspoon salt
¼ cup vegetable oil
1 cup milk
2 eggs, beaten
½ cup taco sauce
2 cups shredded cheddar cheese
1 medium onion, chopped
1 clove garlic, minced
4-ounce can diced green chilies
1 pound ground beef, cooked and drained

In a medium bowl, combine the corn, cornmeal, baking soda, salt, oil, milk, eggs, and taco sauce. Pour half of the mixture into a slow cooker. Layer cheese, onions, garlic, chilies, and ground beef on top of the cornmeal mixture. Cover with remaining cornmeal mixture. Cover. Cook on high for 1 hour, then cook on low for 3 ½ to 4 hours. Or, cook on low for 6 hours.

S. Francie Russell
Meeker, Okla.
Canadian Valley Electric Cooperative

Brazilian Carrot Cake

2 cups carrots, peeled and chopped
½ cup butter
½ cup canola oil
3 eggs
2 cups self-rising flour
1 ½ cups granulated sugar
1 can sweetened condensed milk
1 tablespoon margarine
3 tablespoons sweetened chocolate powder, such as Nesquik, or cocoa powder

Preheat the oven to 350°F. Place the carrots, butter, oil, and eggs into a blender and blend for 5 minutes. In a medium bowl, mix the flour and the sugar. Pour the carrot mixture into the dry ingredients and stir well to combine. Pour the batter into a greased, floured bundt pan. Bake for 40 minutes. While the cake is baking, combine the condensed milk, margarine, and chocolate or cocoa powder in a saucepan. Cook over medium heat, stirring constantly, until the chocolate mixture pulls away from the pan—about 15 minutes. Once the cake is done, allow it to cool for 10 minutes. Loosen it from the pan and invert it onto a plate. Pour the chocolate mixture over the top.

Piettra Alves
Lawton, Okla.

Brigadeiros

Brigadeiros (Brazilian Chocolates)

1 can sweetened condensed milk
1 tablespoon margarine
3 tablespoons sweetened chocolate powder, such as Nesquik, or cocoa powder
chocolate sprinkles

Grease a platter. On another platter, place 40 to 45 1-inch candy liners. Pour the chocolate sprinkles into a shallow bowl. Add the condensed milk, margarine, and chocolate or cocoa powder to a medium saucepan. Cook over medium heat, stirring constantly, until the mixture pulls away from the bottom of the pan (a candy thermometer should read approximately 245°F). Remove from the heat and pour the contents of the saucepan onto the greased platter. Allow the chocolate to stand until it is cool enough to touch. Roll the chocolate into ¾-inch balls and place them in the bowl with the chocolate sprinkles. Roll them in the sprinkles immediately and transfer to the candy liners. Store leftovers in an airtight container.

Anna Politano
Guthrie, Okla.
Oklahoma Living Managing Editor

Chicken Adobo

2 pounds boneless, skinless chicken thighs
1/3 cup soy sauce
1/3 cup rice vinegar
2 bay leaves
1 tablespoon minced garlic
1 teaspoon black peppercorns
1 tablespoon brown sugar

Place all ingredients in a slow cooker and cook on low for 6 to 8 hours, until the meat is tender. Transfer the meat and juices to a large skillet. Bring the liquid to a simmer and reduce by half. Serve with rice.

March 2012
Oklahoma Living

Chicken Adobo

Asian-style Orange Pork

2 oranges
2 tablespoons soy sauce
2 tablespoons rice vinegar
2 tablespoons brown sugar
1 teaspoon red pepper flakes
4 green onions
¼ cup slivered almonds
⅔ cup cornstarch
4 egg whites
1 ½ teaspoons kosher salt
2 pounds boneless pork loin roast, fat trimmed
canola oil for frying

Zest one of the oranges into a small bowl and juice both of the oranges into the bowl. Mix in the soy sauce, vinegar, brown sugar, and red pepper flakes. Slice the green onions into thin pieces and set aside. In a dry skillet, toast the almonds over medium-high heat, shaking the pan frequently so they brown but do not burn. In a medium bowl, combine the cornstarch, egg whites, and ½ teaspoon of the salt. Cut the pork into 1-inch cubes. If the pork is wet, pat it dry with a paper towel. Sprinkle it with the remaining teaspoon of salt. Add the pork to the bowl with the cornstarch batter and mix to coat. To a large skillet over medium-high heat, add enough canola oil to coat the bottom of the pan. Allow the oil to preheat until a drop of the batter sizzles in the skillet. With tongs, place the pork pieces into the skillet so they are not touching one another. Depending on the size of the skillet, the pork may need to be cooked in multiple batches. Cook the pork for approximately 4 minutes, flipping each piece to brown every side. Transfer the cooked pork to a plate lined with paper towels. Add more oil to the skillet as needed. Once all of the pork is cooked, add the orange juice mixture to the skillet. Bring it to a boil and add the pork, green onions, and almonds. Cook for a couple more minutes, until a larger chunk of pork is done in the center. Serve over rice.

April 2011
Oklahoma Living

Asian-style Orange Pork

Pad Thai

½ pound dry rice noodles
3 tablespoons tamarind puree or
 1 tablespoon white vinegar
2 tablespoons unpacked brown sugar
2 ½ tablespoons fish sauce
¼ pound medium shrimp
3 tablespoons vegetable oil
2 eggs
2 tablespoons chopped garlic
¼ pound fresh bean sprouts
3 tablespoons coarsely chopped
 dry-roasted peanuts
3 ounces Chinese chives or green
 onions, cut into 1-inch pieces

Soak the noodles in warm water for 20 minutes; drain. In a small bowl, combine the tamarind puree or vinegar, brown sugar, and fish sauce; set aside. Peel and devein the shrimp. In a wok or large frying pan, heat the oil over medium-high heat. Once heated, swirl the oil to coat the pan. Add the eggs to the pan and lightly scramble. Once the eggs are set, add the shrimp and garlic and sauté until the shrimp is pink. Add the noodles, half of the bean sprouts, half of the peanuts, and the chives, and toss like a salad until fully mixed. Once the noodles are soft, add the sauce and mix to coat evenly. Sprinkle the remaining chopped peanuts on top. Serve with lime wedges and fresh bean sprouts on the side.

Rut Wattanasak
Tulsa, Okla.

Uniquely Oklahoman

Cream Cheese Kolaches

8 ounces cream cheese, softened
1 cup butter
2 cups all-purpose flour
2 egg yolks
1 cup granulated sugar
1 teaspoon baking powder
½ teaspoon vanilla extract
1 to 2 teaspoons filling (fruit,
 cheese, nut, or seed)

Preheat the oven to 400°F. In a medium bowl, mix all ingredients together. Transfer the dough onto a smooth surface and roll into a ¼-inch- to ½-inch-thick sheet. Cut out 1 ½-inch circles. Place the cut dough on a baking sheet and decorate the center with 1 to 2 teaspoons of your favorite filling (such as prune, apricot, cherry, cheese, almond, or poppy seed). Place in a preheated oven and bake for 10 to 12 minutes. Allow to cool and sprinkle lightly with powdered sugar.

October 1995
Oklahoma Living

Thai Omelet

3 tablespoons vegetable oil
4 room-temperature eggs
2 whole green onions, chopped into ¼-inch pieces
1 tablespoon chopped cilantro
¼ pound room-temperature ground pork
½ teaspoon ground white pepper
½ tablespoon fish sauce
½ tablespoon Thai soy sauce

Preheat a frying pan over medium-high heat. Add the oil and allow the skillet to preheat for another 1 to 2 minutes. (The key to a good Thai omelet is a hot pan and oil.) In a bowl, whisk all ingredients together until foam forms on the top. Swirl the pan until it is coated with oil. Add the egg mixture. Allow the eggs to cook until set, about 3 to 5 minutes. Carefully flip the omelet and allow it to cook for another 1 to 3 minutes. Serve with rice and Sriracha sauce.

Rut Wattanasak
Tulsa, Okla.

Thai Omelet

German-style Cabbage and Apples

2 tablespoons butter
⅓ cup finely chopped onion
¼ cup granulated sugar
6 cups shredded red cabbage
½ cup red wine vinegar
1 ½ teaspoons salt
1 large apple, diced
1 ½ cups room-temperature sour cream

Melt the butter in a large skillet over medium-low heat; sauté the onion with 2 tablespoons of the sugar for 5 minutes. Stir in the cabbage, vinegar, and salt; cover and simmer for 20 minutes. Stir in the apples and the remaining 2 tablespoons of sugar; cover and simmer for about 5 minutes. Transfer to a heated serving platter using a slotted spoon. Spoon sour cream over the center of the cabbage. Garnish with apple slices if desired. Serve immediately.

June 1984
Oklahoma Rural News

Beverages

Spiced Hot Chocolate (see page 150).

Spiced Pumpkin Latte

1 tablespoon pumpkin puree
1 tablespoon granulated sugar
1 tablespoon water
¼ teaspoon pumpkin pie spice
1 shot espresso or 1 cup strong coffee
½ cup milk, heated
whipped cream (optional)

In a microwave-safe coffee mug, mix the pumpkin puree, sugar, water, and pumpkin pie spice. Heat in the microwave until it is hot, about 20 seconds. Add the espresso or coffee and stir to combine with the pumpkin mixture. Top with heated milk, whipped cream, and a sprinkle of pumpkin pie spice.

November 2011
Oklahoma Living

Spiced Pumpkin Latte

Caramel Latte

1 or 2 shots of espresso or strong coffee
2 tablespoons vanilla syrup
½ cup heated, frothed milk
whipped cream
caramel sauce

Combine the espresso, vanilla syrup, and frothed milk in a mug. Top with whipped cream and drizzle with caramel sauce.

Caramel Sauce

½ cup heavy cream
1 cup granulated sugar
¼ cup water
1 tablespoon corn syrup
2 tablespoons butter
pinch salt
½ teaspoon vanilla extract

In a small saucepan, heat the heavy cream until it is warm. To a large saucepan, add the sugar, water, and corn syrup. Heat over medium-high heat. The sugar will begin to bubble and turn color. Once it becomes a dark amber color, turn off the heat. Very carefully stir in the warmed heavy cream. The mixture will bubble up. Mix well. If any sugar crystals form, heat the caramel over low heat until they dissolve. Add the butter, salt, and vanilla. Store the cooled caramel sauce in the refrigerator.

Vanilla Syrup

2 cups granulated sugar
2 cups water
1 vanilla bean
1 teaspoon vanilla extract

To a medium saucepan, add the sugar and the water. Split a vanilla bean open lengthwise and use the tip of a sharp knife to scrape the seeds from it. Place the seeds and the pod in the saucepan. Heat the mixture over medium-high, stirring occasionally. Once the sugar dissolves, reduce the heat to a simmer and cook for 10 minutes. Strain the liquid through a wire sieve to remove the pod and stir in the vanilla extract. Store the cooled syrup in the refrigerator.

October 2012
Oklahoma Living

Caramel Latte

Witch's Brew

- ½ cup hot water
- 6 tablespoons cocoa
- 1 ½ cup corn syrup or ½ cup granulated sugar
- ⅛ teaspoon salt
- 1 teaspoon vanilla extract
- 1 cup milk
- marshmallows

In a large saucepan, pour the hot water over the cocoa and stir until smooth. Add the corn syrup or sugar and salt. Simmer for 10 minutes, stirring constantly. Add the vanilla. Add 1 ½ to 2 tablespoons of Witch's Brew to a cup of hot or cold milk. Top with marshmallows. Can also be served hot or cold over ice cream, cottage pudding, or dry cake.

October 1950
Oklahoma Rural News

Apple Cider Tea

- 1 cup apple cider
- 1 teaspoon loose-leaf black tea or 1 bag black tea

Heat apple cider to boiling. Pour over tea leaves or immerse a tea bag. Allow tea to steep according to package instructions. Remove tea bag or leaves before serving.

October 2012
Oklahoma Living

Apple Cider Tea

Mama's Hot Lemonade

"This is a family recipe passed down from my grandmother's family. This hot lemonade is not just great on a cold winter's day, but it's also a great remedy for a sore throat."

2 cups water
1 lemon
6 tablespoons granulated sugar

Add the water to a saucepan. Cut the lemon in half and squeeze the juice into the water; reserve the rind. Add the sugar and stir until it is dissolved. Cut the lemon rind into ¼-inch-thick slices. Add the slices to the water mixture. Cook over medium heat until the mixture begins to simmer. Turn the heat off and put a lid on the pan. Let the lemonade steep for 5 minutes. The rind should be almost transparent. Serve hot. Add some of the lemon rind to each cup.

Pamela Darlene Hargrove
Verdigris Valley Electric Cooperative

Hot Cranberry Tea

3 ½ quarts water
12-ounce package fresh cranberries
2 cups granulated sugar
2 oranges, juiced
2 lemons, juiced
12 whole cloves
2 cinnamon sticks

In a large pot, combine the water and cranberries. Bring the liquid to a boil, reduce the heat, and simmer for 30 minutes. Add the sugar, orange juice, lemon juice, cloves, and cinnamon sticks. Cover and steep for 1 hour.

Mary J. Moerbe
Blackwell, Okla.
Kay Electric Cooperative

Serving tea at the Oklahoma Association of Electric Cooperatives 1968 annual meeting.

Honey and Cinnamon Cold Remedy

1 teaspoon raw honey
¼ teaspoon ground cinnamon

Mix the honey and cinnamon in a small bowl. Take this amount every few hours as soon as you feel a cold coming on.

Barbara Harris
Pocola, Okla.
Arkansas Valley Electric Cooperative

Mulled Cider

2 quarts apple cider
1 lemon, sliced
4 sticks cinnamon
6 whole cloves
¼ teaspoon ground nutmeg
¼ teaspoon powdered ginger

In large saucepan or slow cooker, combine all ingredients. Bring to a boil and reduce the heat to low. Simmer for 30 to 40 minutes; strain. Serve hot.

November 1990
Oklahoma Rural News

Spiced Hot Chocolate

1 cup milk
1 tablespoon cocoa powder
1 ½ tablespoons granulated sugar
⅛ teaspoon vanilla extract
pinch ground cinnamon
smidgen cayenne pepper (optional)

In a small saucepan, whisk together the milk, cocoa powder, and sugar. Heat over medium heat until the milk is warm and the sugar dissolves. Remove from the heat and stir in the vanilla, a pinch of cinnamon, and a smidgen of cayenne pepper, if desired.

October 2012
Oklahoma Living

Cider Punch

1 gallon apple cider
3 cups orange juice
2 cups pineapple juice
1 cup honey
½ cup cinnamon candies, such as Red Hots or 2 cinnamon sticks

Heat all ingredients in a slow cooker; serve.

Michelle Lawson
Perry, Okla.
Central Rural Electric Cooperative

Fruity Punch

3 3-ounce boxes strawberry gelatin
6 cups boiling water
3 cups granulated sugar
1 small frozen lemonade concentrate, thawed
1 small frozen orange juice concentrate, thawed
1 large can pineapple juice
1 gallon cold water
2 bottles ginger ale

Dissolve the gelatin in the boiling water. Add the sugar and stir to dissolve. Stir in the lemonade concentrate, orange juice concentrate, and pineapple juice. Mix and refrigerate. Add the cold water and ginger ale just before serving.

Janice Butz
Sapulpa, Okla.
Indian Electric Cooperative

Cherry Limeade Punch

1 carton cherry limeade sherbet, such as Braum's
2 2-liter bottles lemon-lime soda, such as Sprite

Mix ingredients in a punch bowl; serve.

Cecelia Morford
Oklahoma City, Okla.

Strawberry-Pineapple Punch

- 2 10-ounce packages frozen sliced sweetened strawberries, thawed
- 46-ounce can pineapple juice, chilled
- 4 cups lemon-lime soda, chilled

In food processor or blender, puree the strawberries. Pour into a large punch bowl. Stir in the pineapple juice and soda.

Kathy Kaad
Porter, Okla.
Lake Region Electric Cooperative

Banana-Pineapple Punch

- 4 cups water
- 3 cups granulated sugar
- 46-ounce can pineapple juice
- 1 can frozen orange juice concentrate, thawed
- 2 tablespoons lemon juice
- 5 bananas, mashed
- 2 2-liter bottles ginger ale

Boil the water and sugar for 3 minutes. Cool and add the pineapple juice, orange juice concentrate, and 2 orange juice cans full of water. In a small container, mix the mashed bananas and lemon juice; freeze. To serve, combine all ingredients in a punch bowl.

Lucille Richardson
Oklahoma City, Okla.

THE ELECTRIC FREEZER

A freezer can be a great asset to your home food storage system, home economists say. It allows you to take advantage of special food sale prices and quantity purchases as well as freezing and storing seasonal fruits and vegetables. In addition, taking advantage of your freezer's capabilities can help you cut down on those extra trips to the grocery store to save you time, money and gas.

Oklahoma Rural News
September 1982

The electric freezer is a great way to save on food costs.

Tangy Party Punch

46-ounce can pineapple juice
46-ounce can orange juice
12-ounce frozen limeade concentrate, thawed
12-ounce frozen lemonade concentrate, thawed
3 liters ginger ale
3 pints orange, lime, or lemon sherbet

Pour all liquid ingredients into a punch bowl; mix together. Add the sherbet to the punch by the scoop.

Michelle Lawson
Perry, Okla.
Central Rural Electric Cooperative

Strawberry-Lemon Slush

6-ounce can frozen lemonade
1 pint strawberries, hulled
30 ice cubes

Place all ingredients in a blender and process until smooth.

May 1994
Oklahoma Living

Purple-Power Punch

1 packet blue raspberry drink mix, such as Kool-Aid
1 quart water
1 gallon red Hawaiian punch
1 liter ginger ale
1 pint raspberry sherbet
12 ounces frozen raspberries

Dissolve the drink mix in the water. Combine it with the Hawaiian punch and the ginger ale. Approximately 30 minutes before serving, stir in the sherbet and frozen raspberries.

Sheila Anderson
Lawton, Okla.

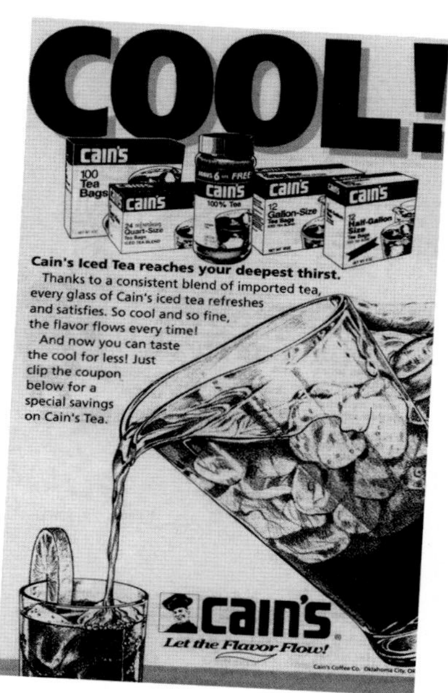

A Cain's iced tea ad from 1991.

Watermelon Lemonade

6 cups cubed watermelon, seeds removed
¼ cup raspberries
1 cup water
⅓ cup granulated sugar
½ cup lemon juice

Place the watermelon, raspberries, and water in a blender; blend until smooth. Strain the mixture through a fine mesh strainer into a pitcher. Stir in the sugar and lemon juice.

August 2001
Oklahoma Living

Uniquely Oklahoman

Watermelon Cooler

2 cups watermelon balls
1 cup blueberries
1 pint lemon sherbet
1 quart ginger ale, chilled

Divide watermelon balls and blueberries among four tall glasses. Add ½ cup of lemon sherbet to each glass. Fill glasses with ginger ale.

August 1979
Oklahoma Rural News

Watermelon Cooler and Watermelon Frosted

Watermelon Frosted

¼ large watermelon
1 pint vanilla ice cream

Cut watermelon into chunks and remove the seeds. Put through a food mill to make 3 cups of clear juice. Divide among four tall glasses. Scoop ½ cup of ice cream into each glass.

August 1979
Oklahoma Rural News

Strawberry-Basil Infused Water

Strawberry-Basil Infused Water

6 strawberries
¼ cup fresh basil leaves
1 pitcher water

Slice the strawberries and place them into a clear glass pitcher with the basil leaves. Add enough water to cover them. Use a wooden spoon to lightly mash the strawberries and bruise the basil leaves. Fill the pitcher with water and place it in the refrigerator for 30 minutes before serving. Serve over ice cubes.

August 2012
Oklahoma Living

Strawberry Milkshake

Strawberry Milkshake

- 1 cup sliced sweetened strawberries
- 1 pint strawberry ice cream
- 1 cup lemon sherbet
- 1 cup milk

Place all ingredients in a blender; blend until smooth and frothy. Serve immediately with additional scoops of ice cream and strawberries for garnish.

August 1984
Oklahoma Rural News

Jan's Summertime Peach Milkshake

3 fresh peaches, peeled and pitted
2 tablespoons granulated sugar
4 ounces milk
1 teaspoon lime juice
4 ice cubes
2 cups vanilla ice cream

Blend all ingredients in a blender until smooth.

Judith Whelchel
Blanchard, Okla.
Oklahoma Electric Cooperative

Lightened-up Eggnog

2 cups fat-free half-and-half
¼ cup granulated sugar
¼ teaspoon ground nutmeg
4 eggs
¾ cup brandy

Heat the half-and-half, sugar, and nutmeg in a medium saucepan to a simmer. Crack the eggs into a blender and blend on low for 1 minute. With the blender running, slowly add the hot cream mixture. Continue blending until frothy, for 30 seconds more. Add the brandy and blend to combine. Serve warm.

Jennifer Dempsey
Oklahoma Association of Electric Cooperatives

Hidden Veggie Smoothie

1 cup water
1 cup ice cubes
fresh fruit (apple, banana, blueberries, strawberries, mango, pineapple, cranberries, cherries, etc.)
handful leafy vegetables (spinach, kale, or collard greens)
1-inch piece fresh ginger, peeled
slice peeled lemon or lime
1 tablespoon flax seed (optional)

Combine all ingredients in a blender and process.

Jackie Whitley
Cherokee, Okla.
Alfalfa Electric Cooperative

Hidden Veggie Smoothie

Desserts

Individual Pavlovas (see page 181).

Martha Washington Candy Balls

1 tablespoon butter, melted
1 cup flaked coconut, such as Baker's Angel Flake
2 cups chopped pecans
1 can sweetened condensed milk
2 pounds powdered sugar
12 ounces milk chocolate chips
¼ pound paraffin (baker's) wax

Combine the butter, coconut, pecans, and condensed milk. Add the powdered sugar; mix well. Form into 1-inch balls. Chill the balls in the refrigerator for 1 to 2 hours. Melt the chocolate chips and wax together in a double boiler. Insert a toothpick into each ball. Dip the balls into the melted chocolate and place on wax paper to cool. Store in a sealed container.

Darlene Sapp
Mustang, Okla.
East Central Oklahoma Electric Cooperative

Window Pane Candy

1 cup milk chocolate chips
1 cup semisweet chocolate chips
½ cup margarine
1 cup flaked coconut
10 ½-ounce package colored miniature marshmallows
1 cup nuts

Melt chips and margarine together; cool. Stir in the coconut, marshmallows, and nuts. Place the mixture onto the center of a sheet of waxed paper. Roll up the sides of the waxed paper to form a log. Refrigerate for at least 3 hours. Cut the log into slices.

Carrie Gosnell
Durant, Okla.
Southeastern Electric Cooperative

Kay's Microwave Peanut Brittle

1 cup granulated sugar
½ cup light corn syrup
1 cup peanuts
1 teaspoon vanilla extract
1 teaspoon butter
2 teaspoons baking soda

In a medium, microwave-safe bowl, mix the sugar, corn syrup, and peanuts. Cook for 4 minutes. Stir and cook for 3 more minutes. Mix in the vanilla and butter. Cook for 2 minutes. Add the baking soda and stir. Pour the mixture into 3 greased pie pans or onto a greased baking sheet. Cool and break into pieces.

Kay Bridges
Apache, Okla.

Mocha Truffles

- 2 12-ounce packages semisweet chocolate chips
- 8 ounces cream cheese, softened
- 3 tablespoons instant coffee granules
- 2 teaspoons water
- 1 pound dark melting chocolate

In a microwave-safe bowl, melt the chocolate chips. Add the cream cheese, coffee, and water. Mix well with an electric mixer. Chill until firm. Form the chilled mixture into 1-inch balls and place on a wax paper-lined baking sheet. Chill for 45 minutes or until firm. Heat the melting chocolate in a microwave-safe bowl. Dip the balls in chocolate and place on wax paper to harden. Store covered in the refrigerator.

Michelle Lawson
Perry, Okla.
Central Rural Electric Cooperative

Buttermilk Fudge

- 2 cups granulated sugar
- ¾ cup buttermilk
- ½ cup light corn syrup

Boil all ingredients together until a few drops will form a soft ball when dropped into cold water. Cool until the side of the saucepan can be touched comfortably. Butter a pie pan or platter. Pour into the buttered container and let stand until firm.

June 1958
Oklahoma Rural News

Peanut Butter Fudge

- 1½ cups chunky peanut butter
- 1 cup margarine
- 1 pound powdered sugar
- 8 chocolate bars, such as Hershey's, melted

Soften peanut butter and margarine in the microwave; stir in the sugar. Press into a 9-by-13-inch pan. Spread the melted chocolate bars on top.

Kay Bamberl
Monkey Island, Okla.
Northeast Oklahoma Electric Cooperative

"Here's to the Red, White, and Blue" Pie

"I entered this recipe in the 2010 Oklahoma State Fair Pie Baking Contest and won first place! It also came in first runner-up in the Pillsbury National Pie Baking Contest. I named the pie 'Here's to the Red, White, and Blue' to honor our military, our flag, and our country. This pie was pictured in the Pillsbury 2012 calendar for the month of July."

2 refrigerated piecrusts, such as Pillsbury
2 tablespoons sugar crystals, such as Wilton White Sparkling Sugar
3 pounds fresh strawberries
1 cup fresh blueberries
¾ cup granulated sugar or ½ cup sugar substitute, such as Splenda
2 tablespoons cornstarch
1½ cups water
3-ounce box strawberry gelatin or sugar-free strawberry gelatin, such as Jell-O

Preheat the oven to 450°F. Place 1 crust in an ungreased 9-inch pie plate (preferably glass). Press the crust firmly against the sides and bottom of the pan. Fold the excess crust under to form a thick crust and flute it. Prick the bottom and sides of the crust with a fork. Unroll the second crust onto wax paper. Use a small star-shaped cookie cutter to cut stars out of the crust. Place the stars on a baking sheet and sprinkle with sugar crystals. Bake the piecrust and stars for 10 to 12 minutes, until light and golden. Cool the crust and transfer the stars to a cooling rack. Wash and hull the strawberries and drain on paper towels with the points facing up. Wash the blueberries and spread them on paper towels to dry. In a saucepan, add the sugar, cornstarch, and water. Bring the mixture to a rolling boil for 2 full minutes. Remove the pan from the heat and add the gelatin, mixing thoroughly. Once the gelatin mixture is cool, stir in the fruit, making sure each piece is coated. Fill the crust with the fruit. Chill for at least 4 hours or overnight. Top with the stars before serving with whipped topping.

"Here's to the Red, White, and Blue" Pie

Janie Lou Dupler
Lawton, Okla.
Cotton Electric Cooperative

A "**Helpful Hint**" from the February 1953 *Oklahoma Rural News*: To keep pecan meats whole, pour boiling water over whole pecans and let stand for 30 minutes before cracking. Meats may then be removed from shells practically whole.

Sour Cream Apple Pie

9-inch pie shell
5 large tart apples, peeled and cored
1 tablespoon lemon juice
¾ cup granulated sugar
¾ cup all-purpose flour
¼ teaspoon salt
1 teaspoon ground cinnamon
¼ teaspoon ground nutmeg
¼ cup butter
½ cup sour cream

Preheat the oven to 400°F. Line a 9-inch pie pan with crust. Cut the apples into thick slices. Arrange them in rows in the pastry-lined pan. Sprinkle them with lemon juice. Combine the dry ingredients; cut in the butter until crumbly. Spoon the mixture over the fruit. Spread the sour cream over the top. Bake for 25 minutes, then reduce the heat to 350°F and bake until the apples are tender, about 20 to 25 minutes longer.

Edl Lee Foster
Lawton, Okla.

Uniquely Oklahoman

Maple Pecan Pie

"This has a very rich flavor with the Aunt Jemima Butter Rich Syrup. Once you try it you won't make a pecan pie any other way."

3 eggs
⅔ cup granulated sugar
½ teaspoon salt
⅓ cup butter, melted
1 cup butter-rich syrup, such as Aunt Jemima
1 cup pecans, broken
9-inch pie shell, unbaked

Preheat the oven to 375°F. Beat the eggs, sugar, salt, butter, and syrup with a hand beater. Stir in the pecans. Pour into the pie shell. Bake until set, for 40 to 50 minutes. Cool slightly. Serve warm or refrigerate.

Janice Storm
South Coffeyville, Okla.

Flaky Pie Crust

2 cups all-purpose flour
1 teaspoon salt
¾ cup butter-flavored shortening
5 tablespoons cold water

Combine the flour and salt in a medium bowl. Cut in the shortening with a pastry blender. Add the cold water and work the dough into a ball. Roll out on a floured surface to fit the pie pan.

Becky Sparks
Blair, Okla.
Southwest Rural Electric Association

Frozen Peanut Butter Pie

Frozen Peanut Butter Pie

4 ounces cream cheese
1 cup powdered sugar
⅓ cup peanut butter
½ cup milk
9 ounces whipped topping
9-inch graham cracker crust or regular
pie crust, baked and cooled
chopped peanuts

Whip the cream cheese until soft and fluffy. Beat in the sugar and peanut butter. Slowly add milk, blending thoroughly into the mixture. Fold in the whipped topping. Pour the filling into the baked and cooled pie shell. Sprinkle with chopped peanuts. Freeze until firm and serve. If not used the same day, wrap in plastic wrap after the pie is frozen. Remove from the freezer about 30 minutes before serving.

March 1984
Oklahoma Rural News

A "**Helpful Hint**" from the October 1954 *Oklahoma Rural News*: Chill your pie dough in the refrigerator for 15 minutes for extra flakiness.

Mom's Chipmunk Pie

½ cup all-purpose flour
1 teaspoon baking powder
¼ teaspoon vanilla extract
¼ teaspoon salt
¾ cup granulated sugar
1 egg
1 cup peeled and chopped apple
½ cup chopped pecans or walnuts

Preheat the oven to 350°F. Mix all ingredients thoroughly. Pour the mixture into a well-greased pie pan and bake for 30 minutes.

Margaret Luttrell
Eufaula, Okla.

Spiced Cupcakes

1 cup all-purpose flour
1 teaspoon baking powder
⅛ teaspoon salt
½ teaspoon ground ginger
¼ teaspoon ground cinnamon
¼ teaspoon ground cloves
½ teaspoon ground allspice
½ teaspoon baking soda
1 egg, beaten
⅓ cup molasses
3 tablespoons granulated sugar
2 pounds melted fat
⅓ cup boiling water
½ cup crushed pineapple, drained

Preheat the oven to 350°F. Sift the flour and measure. In a medium bowl, combine the sifted flour with the baking powder, salt, spices, and baking soda and sift the mixture twice. Mix together the egg, molasses, sugar, melted fat, and water. Add the dry ingredients and stir until just dampened. Add the pineapple. Fill greased muffin tins with the batter. Bake for 20 to 25 minutes. Other fruit or nuts may be used instead of pineapple for variation.

August 1948
Oklahoma Rural News

Lemon Pound Cake

"My youngest brother always requested this for his birthday instead of a regular cake. I still make it today for my family."

1 ½ cups butter, softened
3 cups granulated sugar
5 eggs
3 cups all-purpose flour
2 teaspoons lemon extract
1 teaspoon lemon zest
¾ cup lemon-lime soda

Preheat the oven to 325°F. Cream the butter and sugar until light and fluffy. Add the eggs one at a time, beating well after each addition. Add the remaining ingredients and beat well. Bake in a greased and lightly floured bread or bundt pan for about 1 hour. Cool for 20 to 25 minutes before removing from the pan.

Pamela Leiding
Tonkawa, Okla.
Kay Electric Cooperative

Hot Fudge Cake

For the cake:
½ cup granulated sugar
1 cup self-rising flour
2 tablespoons cocoa powder
3 tablespoons butter, melted
½ cup milk
1 teaspoon vanilla extract

For the topping:
¼ cup granulated sugar
½ cup brown sugar
¼ cup cocoa powder
1 ½ cups hot water

Preheat the oven to 350°F. For the cake, combine the sugar, flour, and cocoa powder in a medium bowl. Blend in the butter, milk, and vanilla. Spread evenly in an 8-inch- or 9-inch-square baking dish. For the topping, combine the dry ingredients in a small bowl and sprinkle the mixture evenly over the cake batter. Drizzle the hot water evenly over the topping. Do not stir. Bake for 45 minutes. Serve warm with a scoop of vanilla ice cream or whipped cream.

Barbara Harris
Pocola, Okla.
Arkansas Valley Electric Cooperative

A "**Helpful Hint**" from the April 1953 *Oklahoma Rural News*: Keep brown sugar from caking and lumping. Put it in a coffee can or airtight plastic bag and store in the refrigerator. It will remain dry and fluffy.

Devil's Food Cake with Caramel Icing

For the cake:
2 cups granulated sugar
½ cup shortening
2 eggs
½ cup buttermilk
3 tablespoons cocoa powder
1 teaspoon baking soda
2 cups all-purpose flour, sifted three times
1 teaspoon vanilla extract
1 cup boiling water

For the caramel icing:
¾ cup granulated sugar
¾ cup brown sugar
½ cup milk or cream
2 tablespoons butter
1 teaspoon vanilla extract

Preheat the oven to 350°F. For the cake, cream the sugar and shortening. Add the eggs and buttermilk; mix. Add the cocoa powder, soda, flour, and vanilla. Mix well and stir in the boiling water. Bake in a greased loaf pan for 40 to 50 minutes or until a toothpick inserted in the center comes out clean. To make the caramel icing, boil the sugars and the milk or cream until the mixture forms a soft ball (234°F). Add the butter and vanilla and beat until the icing reaches a spreading consistency. Ice the cake once it cools.

December 1948
Oklahoma Rural News

Lemon Cake

For the cake:
1 small box lemon gelatin
1 cup boiling water
4 eggs
½ cup oil
1 package yellow cake mix
1 tablespoon lemon extract

For the frosting:
1 cup powdered sugar
3 tablespoons lemon juice
4 tablespoons margarine

Preheat the oven to 350°F. Grease a 9-by-13-inch baking pan. Dissolve the gelatin in the water; set aside to cool. Combine the eggs and oil and beat until fluffy. Add the cake mix and the lemon extract and beat for 3 minutes with an electric mixer. Pour the gelatin mixture in and mix lightly. Transfer the batter to the prepared pan and bake for 30 to 35 minutes or until the cake springs back when touched. Combine the frosting ingredients and spread over the cake while it is hot.

Debbie Hall
Milfay, Okla.
East Central Oklahoma Electric Cooperative

Oklahoma Crude Cake

For the cake:

1 cup granulated sugar
1 cup shortening
4 eggs
1 ½ cups all-purpose flour
¼ teaspoon salt
⅓ cup cocoa powder
1 tablespoon vanilla extract
1 cup chopped pecans (optional)
7-ounce jar marshmallow crème

For the frosting:

⅓ cup cocoa powder
3 ¾ cups powdered sugar
1 cup butter or margarine
⅓ cup evaporated milk
1 teaspoon vanilla extract
1 cup chopped pecans

Preheat the oven to 350°F. Grease a 9-by-13-inch cake pan or two 8-inch round cake pans. In a large bowl, cream together the sugar and shortening. Add the eggs and continue to beat. In a medium bowl, sift together the flour, salt, and cocoa powder. Stir the dry ingredients into the creamed mixture. Add the vanilla and pecans. Pour the batter into the prepared pan and bake for 25 to 30 minutes. Remove the cake from the oven. While it is still hot, spread the marshmallow crème over the top. While the cake is cooling, prepare the frosting. In a mixer bowl, combine the cocoa powder and powdered sugar. Add the butter or margarine, evaporated milk, and vanilla and beat with an electric mixer until the frosting is fluffy. Mix in the pecans. Spread the icing on top of the marshmallow layer.

January 2012
Oklahoma Living

Blue-Ribbon Pumpkin-Pecan Cake

1 box yellow cake mix, such as Duncan Hines
⅓ cup oil
15-ounce can pumpkin
¾ cup granulated sugar
¼ cup water
4 eggs
1 teaspoon ground cinnamon
⅛ teaspoon ground nutmeg
1 cup chopped pecans

Preheat the oven to 350°F. In a medium bowl, mix all of the ingredients together, blending well. Pour the mixture into a greased and floured bundt pan and bake for 1 hour.

Louise Brandenburg
Fairfax, Okla.
Indian Electric Cooperative

Molten Chocolate Cake

1 tablespoon cocoa powder
¼ cup plus 1 tablespoon all-purpose flour
10 ounces bittersweet chocolate
¼ cup heavy cream
½ cup butter
½ cup granulated sugar
3 room-temperature eggs
1 teaspoon vanilla extract
pinch salt
1 tablespoon powdered sugar

Position a baking rack in the center of the oven; preheat the oven to 425°F. Grease four ramekins. In a small bowl, mix the cocoa powder and 1 tablespoon of the flour. Dust the ramekins with the cocoa mixture and place them on a baking sheet. In a double boiler over simmering water, melt 4 ounces of the chocolate and mix in the heavy cream. Once combined, chill the mixture. In a small saucepan over low heat, melt the butter and the remaining 6 ounces of chocolate, stirring occasionally. Allow the mixture cool. To a mixer bowl, add the granulated sugar and eggs. Beat with an electric mixer on medium-high speed for about 3 minutes, until the mixture is a pale yellow color. Fold the melted chocolate and butter mixture into the egg mixture. Add the vanilla and fold in the remaining ¼ cup of flour and the salt. Spoon the chocolate batter into the four ramekins, reserving a third of the batter. From the chilled chocolate and cream mixture, form four balls. Place one ball in the center of each ramekin. Spoon the rest of the batter into the ramekins. Place the baking sheet onto the center rack of the oven. Bake for approximately 16 minutes, until the tops crack. The centers will be slightly soft. Let the cakes cool for 5 minutes, then use a knife to loosen the cakes from the ramekins. Invert each cake onto a plate and sprinkle with powdered sugar. Serve warm with ice cream.

February 2011
Oklahoma Living

Molten Chocolate Cake

A "**Helpful Hint**" from the April 1953 *Oklahoma Rural News*: To prepare cake tins, use lard, vegetable shortening or salad oil rather than butter. The water and salt in the cake are likely to make the cake sticky.

Carrot-Pineapple Cake with Cream Cheese Icing

For the cake:
2 cups grated carrot
2 cups granulated sugar
1 ½ cups vegetable oil
4 eggs
2 cups all-purpose flour
2 teaspoons baking soda
1 teaspoon salt
1 teaspoon ground cinnamon
1 small can crushed pineapple, undrained

For the icing:
8 ounces cream cheese
¼ cup butter
1 pound powdered sugar
1 teaspoon vanilla extract
½ cup nuts

Preheat the oven to 350°F. Line the bottoms of three 8-inch round pans with parchment; grease and flour the pans. In a large bowl, combine the carrot, sugar, and oil. Add the eggs one at a time, beating well after each addition. In a medium bowl, sift together the flour, baking soda, salt, and cinnamon. Add the dry ingredients to the wet ingredients and stir in the pineapple. Divide evenly among the three prepared pans. Bake for approximately 35 minutes. While the cake is baking, make the icing. Cream together the cream cheese and butter in a medium bowl. Add the powdered sugar, vanilla, and nuts. Ice the cooled cake between the layers only.

Janna Boren, former Oklahoma First Lady
April 1975
Oklahoma Rural News

Candy Bar Ice Cream

8 candy bars, such as Milky Way
½ cup milk
5 eggs
1 cup granulated sugar
1 can condensed milk
1 tablespoon vanilla extract
¼ teaspoon salt
1 quart half-and-half

Place the candy bars and milk into a heavy saucepan over low heat and cook until the candy is melted. Beat the eggs and sugar in a medium bowl. Add the remaining ingredients and the candy mixture and continue beating until well mixed. Pour into an ice cream freezer and add enough additional milk to reach 1 inch from the top. Freeze according to manufacturer instructions.

Anne Williams
Vinita, Okla.
KAMO Power

Carrot Cake

For the cake:
3 cups grated carrot
2 cups all-purpose flour
2 cups granulated sugar
2 teaspoons baking soda
1 teaspoon baking powder
½ teaspoon salt
1 teaspoon ground cinnamon
4 eggs, beaten
1 ¼ cup vegetable oil
1 teaspoon vanilla extract

For the frosting:
16-ounce package powdered sugar
8-ounce package cream cheese, softened
½ cup butter or margarine, softened
1 teaspoon vanilla extract
1 cup chopped pecans

Preheat the oven to 350°F. In a medium bowl, combine the carrot, flour, sugar, baking soda, baking powder, salt, and cinnamon; stir in the eggs, oil, and vanilla, mixing well. Spoon the batter into three greased and floured 8-inch cake pans. Bake for 30 minutes or until a toothpick inserted in center of the cake comes out clean. Cool on a cooling rack. To make the frosting, combine the powdered sugar, cream cheese, butter or margarine, and vanilla until well blended, then stir in the pecans. Spread the frosting between each layer and on top and on the sides of the cake.

Elaine Rose Hrdy-Straka
Oklahoma City, Okla.
Oklahoma Electric Cooperative

Baked Indian Pudding

¼ cup cornmeal
5 cups milk
¼ cup molasses
½ teaspoon salt
⅛ teaspoon ground ginger
¼ teaspoon ground cinnamon
1 tablespoon shortening

Preheat the oven to 275°F. In a medium bowl, mix the cornmeal with 1 cup of the milk. Scald the remaining milk in a double boiler or over hot water. Add the cornmeal mixture and the remaining ingredients. Mix well. Pour into a greased baking pan and bake for approximately 2 hours.

October 1982
Oklahoma Rural News

Lemon-Orange Ice Cream

"My grandfather, John A. Woods, came to the land lottery in 1901, and drew a quarter section of farming land here in Comanche County, which was then Indian Territory. His 160 acres have been passed down through the generations and Cotton Electric Cooperative has always furnished the farm with electricity. This recipe was passed down and the only difference is we no longer raise our own cows and chickens to furnish most of the ingredients."

4 eggs
3 cups granulated sugar
4 lemons, zested and juiced
6 oranges, zested and juiced
4 cups heavy cream
6 cups half-and-half

Separate the egg yolks and whites into two separate medium bowls. With a mixer, beat the sugar and egg yolks. Zest the lemons and oranges into another bowl and reserve ½ cup of the zest. Juice all of the lemons and oranges into a bowl and stir the juice into the egg yolk mixture. With clean beaters, beat the egg whites until soft peaks form. Combine the egg yolk mixture with the cream; stir in the citrus zest and fold in the egg whites. Pour the mixture into a large ice cream freezer. Add enough half-and-half to reach the freezer's fill-line. Freeze according to manufacturer instructions.

Janie Lou Dupler
Lawton, Okla.
Cotton Electric Cooperative

Uniquely Oklahoman

Grape Dumplings

1 cup all-purpose flour
1 ½ teaspoons baking powder
2 teaspoons granulated sugar
¼ teaspoon salt
1 tablespoon shortening
½ cup grape juice
additional grape juice for cooking

In a medium bowl, mix the flour, baking powder, sugar, salt, and shortening. Add the grape juice and mix into a stiff dough. Roll the dough very thin on a floured board and cut into ½-inch strips (or roll the dough in hands and break off pea-size bits). Drop into boiling grape juice and cook for 10 to 12 minutes.

The Cherokee Nation

Uniquely Oklahoman

Vinegar Cobbler

"This recipe was given to me by my mom who was born in Willis, Okla., in 1919. It was one of her favorite recipes especially in the early '40s. She always called it her substitute for apple cobbler. The recipe was probably passed down from her mom who was born in Powell, Indian Territory in 1897."

1 ½ cups granulated sugar
½ cup plus 2 tablespoons vinegar
¾ cup butter
3 cups water
1 ½ cups all-purpose flour
½ cup shortening
½ teaspoon salt

Preheat the oven to 375°F. Combine the sugar, vinegar, butter, and water in a large saucepan and bring to a boil. In a bowl, combine the flour, shortening, salt, and enough additional water to form a tough dough. Roll out half of the dough and cut it into strips. Drop them into the boiling mixture. Once the mixture returns to a boil, transfer it to a large baking dish. Roll the remaining dough out and place it on top of the hot mixture. Sprinkle with a generous amount of sugar. Bake for 35 to 45 minutes until the dough is golden brown. Serve hot with ice cream.

Sonja Lowe
Carnegie, Okla.
Caddo Electric Cooperative

Pineapple Delight

8 ounces cream cheese
1 can condensed milk, such as Eagle Brand
⅓ cup lemon juice
1 large can crushed pineapple, drained
1 medium container whipped topping, such as Cool Whip
1 cup chopped pecans
2 9-inch graham cracker pie shells

Place the cream cheese and condensed milk in a large bowl. Mix with an electric mixer until well blended. Stir in the lemon juice. (Batter will become thicker.) Fold in the pineapple, whipped topping, and pecans. Divide evenly between the 2 pie shells and chill before serving.

Lou Gray
Lindsay, Okla.
Rural Electric Cooperative

Individual Pavlovas

2 room-temperature egg whites
pinch salt
¼ teaspoon cream of tartar
½ teaspoon cornstarch
6 tablespoons granulated sugar
1 teaspoon vanilla extract
1 cup fresh berries
¼ cup heavy cream
1 ½ teaspoons powdered sugar

Place an oven rack in the middle of the oven and preheat the oven to 250°F. Line a baking sheet with parchment or a silicone baking liner. Starting on low speed and gradually increasing to medium, beat together the egg whites, salt, and cream of tartar with an electric mixer using the whisk attachment until soft peaks form, about 2 to 3 minutes. Add the cornstarch and the sugar 1 tablespoon at a time. Increase the mixer speed to medium-high and beat until stiff peaks form, about 4 to 5 minutes. Mix in ½ teaspoon of the vanilla. Spoon or pipe the mixture into two 4-inch circles onto the baking sheet. Make an indentation in the middle of each meringue to hold the topping. Bake for approximately 75 minutes, until the meringues are crisp on the outside, but still white in color. Carefully remove the meringues from the baking sheet and allow them to cool on a cooling rack. While they are cooling, cut the berries into bite-size pieces. In a chilled medium bowl, whip the heavy cream until stiff peaks almost form. Add the powdered sugar and the remaining ½ teaspoon of vanilla and beat until stiff peaks form. Spoon the heavy cream onto the cooled meringues and top with fruit.

March 2013
Oklahoma Living

Strawberry Yum-Yum

For the crust:
1 cup all-purpose flour
¼ cup brown sugar
½ cup margarine
½ cup chopped nuts

For the filling:
10-ounce package frozen strawberries, thawed
2 egg whites
1 cup granulated sugar
2 teaspoons lemon juice
12 ounces whipped topping, such as Cool Whip

Preheat the oven to 375°F. For the crust, combine the flour, brown sugar, margarine, and chopped nuts and mix until crumbly. Spread in a shallow pan. Bake until golden brown, stirring often. Let cool. Spread half of the cooked crust in the bottom of a 9-by-15-inch baking pan. To make the filling, combine all of the ingredients, except the whipped topping, in a large bowl. Mix slowly with an electric mixer until well blended. Turn the mixer to high speed and mix for 15 to 20 minutes. Fold in the whipped topping. Pour the mixture over the crust. Top with the reserved crumbs. Freeze. (Can be frozen for up to two weeks.)

Cheryl Poe
Cherokee, Okla.
Alfalfa Electric Cooperative

Country Apple Cobbler

"Another Country Apple Cobbler prepared by Mary Ann King, a Verdigris Valley Electric Cooperative employee, comes from the oven. It won't last long as Verdigris Valley employees, family members and friends all brag on her cobbler."

1 cup granulated sugar
2 tablespoons instant tapioca
½ teaspoon ground cinnamon
¼ cup water
¼ cup chopped walnuts and/or raisins
6 cups peeled, thinly sliced apples
½ teaspoon salt
1 ½ teaspoons baking powder
1 ½ cups shredded sharp cheddar cheese
½ cup margarine, melted
½ cup milk

Preheat the oven to 375°F. Combine the sugar, tapioca, cinnamon, and water in a saucepan. Add the walnuts and/or raisins. Cook, stirring constantly, until the mixture boils. Remove from the heat and stir in the apples. Pour the mixture into an 8-inch-square baking dish. In a medium bowl, sift together the salt and baking powder. Stir in the shredded cheese. Add the margarine and milk. Mix until just moistened. Spoon over the apple mixture. Bake for 35 to 40 minutes or until golden brown. Serve warm with whipped topping.

August 1982
Oklahoma Rural News

Persimmon Pudding

2 pounds wild persimmons
2 cups granulated sugar
½ cup butter, melted
1 cup seedless raisins
2 cups all-purpose flour, sifted
¼ teaspoon salt
2 teaspoons baking soda
1 teaspoon ground cinnamon
1 teaspoon ground ginger
½ teaspoon ground nutmeg
1 cup milk
4 teaspoons vanilla extract
1 cup heavy cream, whipped

Preheat the oven to 350°F. Wash, peel, and remove the seeds from the persimmons. Puree the fruit through a sieve or use a blender or food processor. Stir in the sugar, butter, and raisins. Sift together the flour, salt, baking soda, and spices. Add the dry mixture to the persimmon mixture alternately with the milk and vanilla. Spread the batter into a greased 2-quart baking dish. Bake for 50 minutes or until a toothpick inserted in the center comes out clean. Top with whipped cream and serve hot.

December 1982
Oklahoma Rural News

PERSIMMON PUDDING, PERHAPS?

Hard times tend to make people turn to the resources at hand in order to survive. Sit down at their table at mealtime and you might find rabbit stew, fried catfish, persimmon pudding, wild grape jelly or some other dish prepared from what ever was available for the taking.

Oklahomans are finding the current economic slump a time to make-do just as their parents or grandparents did in the '30s, but one who didn't need a recession to make use of the many persimmons at hand this time of year is Johnnie Johnston. Johnnie, a retired nurse and wife of Oliver Johnston, a Kiamichi Electric Cooperative employee, grew up with persimmons, picking them as a child and learning from her mother how to make delicious persimmon dishes.

This is a good persimmon year in eastern Oklahoma and Johnnie and her daughter, Sue Pahlon, are taking advantage of it by making Persimmon Pudding (see page 182), Persimmon Date Nut Bread (see page 37) and a number of other dishes from this product of the wild.

"Times were hard when I was growing up and we used everything, hickory nuts, black walnuts, persimmons and whatever else the land had to offer."

The land wasn't cleared as much then as it is now with people farming during the summer and hunting in the winter to get by.

"Persimmon thickets were where we could go to find furbearing animals and wild turkeys," Oliver said. "I can remember my dad making what he called 'persimmon beer,' but I would say it was more of a tonic."

A lot of people who aren't all that familiar with persimmons think of them as something that will make your mouth pucker when you bite into one. They will if the persimmon is green. A ripe persimmon, on the other hand, is sweet to the taste and it doesn't take many to satisfy one's appetite. Ripe persimmons are a little wrinkled on the outside and are orange to yellow in color.

Oliver, who enjoys fishing, as does Johnnie, has also found that persimmons make good catfish bait. He learned this by finding persimmon seeds among the stomach contents of some catfish he caught a few years ago. This knowledge has served Oliver well in his fall fishing ventures since then as he baits his trotlines with persimmons.

Johnnie and Sue are both active in the Rocky Point Extension Homemakers Group, which has a potluck dinner at each month's meeting. They take persimmon dishes to these dinners during this time of year. Johnnie suggests looking for persimmons that are "firm, not bruised and which don't have black spots" when picking them to make a taste-pleasing dish.

Oklahoma Rural News
December 1982

Banana Split Trifle with Butter-Rum Glaze

For the pound cake:
1 cup unsalted butter, softened
2 cups powdered sugar
3 eggs
1 teaspoon imitation rum extract
1 ½ cups all-purpose flour
¼ teaspoon salt

For the butter-rum glaze:
¼ cup brown sugar
¼ cup granulated sugar
½ cup unsalted butter, softened
2 tablespoons water
½ teaspoon imitation rum extract

For the pudding and fruit layers:
3.4-ounce box banana cream-flavored instant pudding
2 cups cold milk
15-ounce can pineapple chunks, drained
16-ounce container fresh strawberries, washed, hulled, and quartered
8-ounce container whipped topping, thawed
maraschino cherries

Preheat the oven to 325°F. To make the pound cake, cream the butter and powdered sugar in a large bowl until light and fluffy. Add the eggs one at a time, beating well after each addition. Stir in the rum extract. Combine the flour and salt and gradually add to the creamed mixture until just combined. Pour into a greased and floured 8-by-4-inch loaf pan. Bake for 1 hour or until done. Let cool for about 15 minutes before removing the cake from the pan and placing on a cooling rack. Cool completely, then cut into 1-inch cubes. To make the butter-rum glaze, mix the sugars, butter, and water in a medium saucepan over medium heat. Bring the mixture to a boil, stirring constantly. Boil for 3 minutes. Remove from the heat and stir in the rum extract; set aside. Prepare pudding according to package directions. To assemble the trifle, use a trifle bowl or large clear glass bowl. For the first layer, use half of the cubed cake pieces, then drizzle half of the butter-rum glaze over them. Layer on half of the pineapple chunks and half of the chopped strawberries. Top with half of the pudding, then half of the whipped topping. Repeat in the same order. Finish with a layer of whipped topping and decorate with maraschino cherries. Cover and refrigerate for 2 to 3 hours or until chilled.

Angela Sandersfield
Guthrie, Okla.
Cimarron Electric Cooperative

Strawberry Party Tarts

For the tart shells:
2 cups all-purpose flour
1 teaspoon salt
¾ cup shortening
¼ cup cold water

For the tart filling:
3 ounces cream cheese
2 tablespoons thin cream
1 quart fresh strawberries, washed and hulled
1 cup granulated sugar
3 tablespoons cornstarch
1 cup heavy cream, whipped

Preheat the oven to 450°F. To make the tart shells, mix the flour and salt together. Cut in ⅔ cup of the shortening with a pastry blender or two knives until the mixture is as fine as meal. Cut in the remaining shortening until it resembles large peas. Sprinkle the water evenly over the mixture. Mix thoroughly with a fork until the particles cling together and form a ball of dough. Roll the dough out ⅛-inch thick and prick with a fork. Cut into 5-inch rounds and fit over the cups on the underside of a muffin pan, pinching the dough into about seven pleats. Bake for 10 to 15 minutes. Soften the cream cheese with the cream and spread in the bottoms of the baked tart shells. Mash enough berries to make ⅓ cup of strained juice. Cut the remaining berries in half and arrange them on the cheese mixture in the tart shells. Heat the juice to boiling. Combine the sugar and cornstarch and slowly stir into the juice. Cook until clear and thickened, about 10 minutes, stirring occasionally. Let cool. Blend with berry pulp leftover from the strained juice and pour over the berries in the tart shells. Chill until firm. Spread whipped cream over the filling. Chill before serving.

May 1954
Oklahoma Rural News

Apple Carmelina

5 Granny Smith apples, peeled
1 cup granulated sugar
ground cinnamon
1 box yellow cake mix
½ cup butter
caramel sauce

Preheat the oven to 350°F. Core and slice the apples. Place them in a 9-by-13-inch baking pan. Sprinkle the sugar and cinnamon evenly over the apples. In a medium bowl, combine the cake mix and butter until crumbly. Spread the cake mixture over the apples. Bake until the cake is golden brown. Remove from the oven and drizzle caramel sauce over the top. Serve with vanilla ice cream.

Diana Ryals
Cookson, Okla.
Ozarks Electric Cooperative

Index

Apples
- Apple Carmelina, 185
- Country Apple Cobbler, 182
- German-style Cabbage and Apples, 143
- Hidden Veggie Smoothie, 157
- Mom's Chipmunk Pie, 172
- Paper Bag Apple Pie, 168
- Raw Cranberry Relish, 86
- Sour Cream Apple Pie, 170
- Sweet Potato-Apple Delight, 99

Artichokes
- Artichoke Chicken and Olives, 119
- Hearts 'n' Caps, 98

Asian
- Asian Chicken Noodle Soup, 64
- Asian-style Orange Pork, 141
- Pad Thai, 142
- Thai Omelet, 143

Asparagus
- Asparagus Summer Salad, 77
- Sautéed Asparagus with Bacon, 101

Bacon
- Aunt Florrie's Cornbread Salad, 79
- Bacon-Cheeseburger Meatloaf, 110
- Broccoli-Cranberry Salad, 82
- Corn and Wild Onions, 126
- Deviled Egg Balls, 56
- Double-Baked Potato Casserole, 93
- Fried Hominy, 92
- German Sauerkraut, 101
- Ham 'n' Beans, 91
- Hash Brown Potato Casserole, 94
- Layered BLT Dip, 53
- Melissa's Bacon-Ranch Crescents, 18
- Mini Twice-Baked Potatoes, 58
- Really Good Baked Beans, 92
- Sautéed Asparagus with Bacon, 101
- Texhoma Beans, 93

Bananas
- Banana-Pineapple Punch, 152
- Banana Split Trifle with Butter-Rum Glaze, 184
- Double Orange Gelatin Salad, 79
- Healthy Black Bean Brownies, 165
- Hidden Veggie Smoothie, 157

Beans
- Angela's Tamale Soup, 66
- Bean Bread, 30
- Broccoli Salad, 77
- Cheesy Chili Mac, 130
- Chicken Fiesta Soup, 65
- Chicken Tostadas, 135
- Chopped Summer Salad, 83
- Daddy Jim's Taco Soup, 66
- Ham 'n' Beans, 91
- Healthy Black Bean Brownies, 165
- Josh's Chili, 70
- Mexi-Chili Casserole, 128
- Pumpkin, White Bean, and Sausage Stew, 71
- Really Good Baked Beans, 92
- Triple Bean Chowder, 72
- White Christmas Chili, 70

Beef
- Bacon-Cheeseburger Meatloaf, 110
- BBQ Beef Brisket, 112
- Beef Kabobs, 114
- Beef-Stuffed Tomatoes, 116
- Brazilian Stroganoff, 136
- Carolee's Barbeque Brisket, 117
- Company Casserole, 126
- Corned Beef Hash, 17
- Crescent Dinner Roll Lasagna, 107
- Daddy Jim's Taco Soup, 66
- Easy Lasagna, 108
- Favorite Meatloaf, 110
- Grandma's Corned Beef Salad, 82
- Grandma's Meatballs, 111
- Hamburger Stuffed in French Bread, 112
- Jo's Beef Empanadas, 136
- Josh's Chili, 70
- Mark's Favorite Upside-Down Pizza, 109
- Mexi-Chili Casserole, 128
- Mexican Cornbread, 138
- Nacho Cheese Chowder, 73
- Nana Lou's Meatballs, 49
- Pseudo-Enchiladas, 128
- Red Dirt Chili, 69
- River's Bend Short Ribs, 115
- Slow-cooked Cube Steak with Gravy, 113
- Slow Cooker Beef and Potato Stew, 71
- Stir-fried Beef and Grain Salad, 81
- Sweet and Spicy Meatballs, 50
- Taco Pasta, 109
- Tamale Pie, 134
- Tangy Meatballs, 49
- Texhoma Beans, 93
- Western Casserole, 130

Biscuits
- 7-Up Biscuits, 40
- Crispy Whole-Wheat Drop Biscuits, 39
- Dutch Oven Sourdough Biscuits, 41
- Honey Poppy Seed Biscuits, 42
- Land Run Sweet Biscuits, 39
- Sweet Potato Biscuits, 40

Blueberries
- "Here's to the Red, White, and Blue" Pie, 169
- Hidden Veggie Smoothie, 157
- Individual Pavlovas, 181
- Watermelon Cooler, 154
- Yogurt-Berry Parfait, 25

Breads, Quick
- Bean Bread, 30
- Carrot Bread, 29
- Cheesy Pear Nut Bread, 31
- Citrus Nut Bread, 32
- Cranberry-Orange Bread, 30
- Hoe Bread, 34
- Orange Bread, 33

Persimmon Date Nut Bread, 37
Zucchini Bread, 32
Breads, Yeast
Beer Bread, 36
Challah Bread, 35
Dehl Twins' Monkey Bread, 19
Fly-Off-the-Plate Hot Rolls, 38
Fried Indian Bread, 34
Grandpa Veith's Oatmeal Bread, 33
No-Knead Whole-Wheat Bread, 35
Sourdough Starter, 41
Spoon Hot Rolls, 37
Breakfast Casseroles
Breakfast Lasagna, 15
Linda's Breakfast Casserole, 13
Mini Egg Casseroles, 17
Panhandle Casserole, 14
Broccoli
Best-Ever Broccoli Casserole, 96
Broccoli Casserole, 101
Broccoli-Cranberry Salad, 82
Broccoli Salad, 77
Creamy Broccoli Orzo Soup, 63
Fish Fillets over Zesty Lemon Rice, 123
Brownies
Healthy Black Bean Brownies, 165
Mocha Truffle Brownies, 164
Brussels Sprouts
Shredded Brussels Sprouts with Pecans and Mustard Seeds, 99
Cabbage
Chicken and Veggie Salad, 81
German Sauerkraut, 101
German-style Cabbage and Apples, 143
Cakes
Banana Split Trifle with Butter-Rum Glaze, 184
Blue-Ribbon Pumpkin-Pecan Cake, 175
Brazilian Carrot Cake, 138
Carrot Cake, 178
Carrot-Pineapple Cake with Cream Cheese Icing, 177
Devil's Food Cake with Caramel Icing, 174
Hot Fudge Cake, 173
Lemon Cake, 174
Lemon Pound Cake, 173
Molten Chocolate Cake, 176
Oklahoma Crude Cake, 175
Spiced Cupcakes, 172
Candies
Brigadeiros (Brazilian Chocolates), 139
Buttermilk Fudge, 160
Kay's Microwave Peanut Brittle, 159
Martha Washington Candy Balls, 159
Mocha Truffles, 160
Peanut Butter Fudge, 160
Pecan Toffee, 161
Window Pane Candy, 159
Canning
Citrus Marmalade, 26
Pickled Peppers, 103
Sand Plum Jelly, 25
Sliced Zucchini Pickles, 103
Caramel
Apple Carmelina, 185
Caramel Latte, 146
Caramel Sauce, 146
Devil's Food Cake with Caramel Icing, 174
Hardeman Guest House Caramel French Toast, 23
Carrots
Brazilian Carrot Cake, 138
Carrot Bread, 29
Carrot Cake, 178
Carrot-Pineapple Cake with Cream Cheese Icing, 177
Marcie's Carrot Bars, 162
Roasted Country Vegetables, 97
Sweet Carrot Casserole, 96
Casseroles
Best-Ever Broccoli Casserole, 96
Betty Moe's Mexican Chicken Casserole, 129
Broccoli Casserole, 101
Company Casserole, 126
Double-Baked Potato Casserole, 93
Ham and Mushroom Casserole, 131
Hash Brown Potato Casserole, 94
Mexi-Chili Casserole, 128
Praline Sweet Potato Casserole, 95
Sausage and Rice Casserole, 126
Sausage, Squash, and Pecan Casserole, 100
Sweet Carrot Casserole, 96
Western Casserole, 130
Cauliflower
Roasted Country Vegetables, 97
Cheese
Bacon-Cheeseburger Meatloaf, 110
Baked Brie in Puff Pastry, 59
Cheese Muffins, 44
Cheesy Chicken Chowder, 74
Cheesy Chili Mac, 130
Cheesy Garlic-Dill Toast, 36
Cheesy Pear Nut Bread, 31
Four-Cheese Pasta Florentine, 105
Goat Cheese, Pesto, and Pine Nut Bruschetta, 61
King Ranch Chicken Mac and Cheese, 89
Nacho Cheese Chowder, 73
Oklahoma Cheese Toast, 36
Ola Manns' Mac and Cheese, 89
Tomato, Basil, and Fresh Mozzarella Salad, 84
White Queso, 54
Cheese Balls
Chocolate Chip Cheese Ball, 51
Ham and Cheese Ball, 50
Cherry
Cherry Limeade Punch, 151
Cherry Party Salad, 77
Cherry Scones, 43
Hidden Veggie Smoothie, 157
Chicken
Artichoke Chicken and Olives, 119
Asian Chicken Noodle Soup, 64
Betty Moe's Mexican Chicken Casserole, 129
Brazilian Stroganoff, 136
Buffalo Chicken Dip, 53
Cheesy Chicken Chowder, 74
Chicken Adobo, 140
Chicken and Veggie Salad, 81
Chicken-Corn Chowder, 73
Chicken Fiesta Soup, 65

Chicken Spaghetti, 106
Chicken Tostadas, 135
Coconut-Orange Chicken Fajitas, 135
Cornmeal Oven-fried Chicken, 121
Crescent Chicken Squares, 121
Herbed Chicken, 120
Honey BBQ Chicken, 122
Jill's Favorite Tortilla Soup, 64
Johnny's Chicken Salad, 78
King Ranch Chicken Mac and Cheese, 89
Lemon Chicken, 118
Lila Clay's Chicken and Rice, 122
Odie Bob's Chicken and Rice, 122
Slow Cooker Chicken Noodle Soup, 63
Teriyaki Chicken, 120
White Christmas Chili, 70
White Lasagna, 106
Chili
Cheesy Chili Mac, 130
Josh's Chili, 70
Mexi-Chili Casserole, 128
Red Dirt Chili, 69
White Christmas Chili, 70
Chocolate
Brazilian Carrot Cake, 138
Brigadeiros (Brazilian Chocolates), 139
Candy Bar Ice Cream, 177
Chocolate Chip Cheese Ball, 51
Chocolate Gravy, 27
Devil's Food Cake with Caramel Icing, 174
Healthy Black Bean Brownies, 165
Hot Fudge Cake, 173
Martha Washington Candy Balls, 159
Mexican Brunch Chocolate, 134
Mocha Truffle Brownies, 164
Mocha Truffles, 160
Molten Chocolate Cake, 176
Oklahoma Crude Cake, 175
Peanut Butter Fudge, 160
Pecan Toffee, 161
Spiced Hot Chocolate, 150
Window Pane Candy, 159
Witch's Brew, 148
Cider
Apple Cider Tea, 148
Cider Punch, 151
Mulled Cider, 150
Cobblers
Country Apple Cobbler, 182
Vinegar Cobbler, 180
Coconut
Carrot Bread, 29
Cherry Party Salad, 77
Citrus-Coconut Squares, 164
Coconut-Orange Chicken Fajitas, 135
Martha Washington Candy Balls, 159
Window Pane Candy, 159
Coffee
Caramel Latte, 146
Grandma Grof's Oatmeal Cookies, 165
Mocha Truffle Brownies, 164
Mocha Truffles, 160
Spiced Pumpkin Latte, 145
Coffee Cakes
Cream Cheese Coffee Cake, 19
Guam Coffee Cake, 18
Cookies
Citrus-Coconut Squares, 164
Grandma Grof's Oatmeal Cookies, 165
Lemon Bars, 162
Lemon Wrinkles, 163
Marcie's Carrot Bars, 162
Snickerdoodles, 161
Corn
Cheesy Chicken Chowder, 74
Chicken and Veggie Salad, 81
Chicken-Corn Chowder, 73
Chicken Fiesta Soup, 65
Chopped Summer Salad, 83
Corn and Wild Onions, 126
Corn Cob Jelly, 27
Corn Fritters, 92
Cowboy Caviar, 48
Delta's Funeral Salad, 85
Fried Hominy, 92
Grilled Corn, Avocado, and Tomato Salad with Honey-Lime Dressing, 80
Mexican Cornbread, 138
Nacho Cheese Chowder, 73
Scalloped Corn, 90
Slow Cooker Beef and Potato Stew, 71
Tamale Pie, 134
Tanshpashofa, 131
Cornbread
Lydia Wade's Cornbread, 29
Mexican Cornbread, 138
Cornmeal
Baked Indian Pudding, 178
Bean Bread, 30
Classic Fried Catfish, 124
Cornmeal Oven-fried Chicken, 121
Lydia Wade's Cornbread, 29
Mexican Cornbread, 138
Tamale Pie, 134
Cranberries
Baked Brie in Puff Pastry, 59
Broccoli-Cranberry Salad, 82
Cranberry-Orange Bread, 30
Dee's Cranberry Salad, 85
Hidden Veggie Smoothie, 157
Hot Cranberry Tea, 149
Raw Cranberry Relish, 86
Turkey Cranberry Braid, 56
Crescent Rolls
Breakfast Lasagna, 15
Crescent Chicken Squares, 121
Crescent Dinner Roll Lasagna, 107
Linda's Breakfast Casserole, 13
Melissa's Bacon-Ranch Crescents, 18
Turkey Cranberry Braid, 56
Dips
Buffalo Chicken Dip, 53
Jalapeño Popper Spread, 55
Layered BLT Dip, 53
Onion Soufflé, 52
Pineapple Spread, 56
Ray B's Dip, 54
Spicy Spinach Dip, 55
White Queso, 54
Zesty Italian Veggie Dip, 54
Donuts
Easy Donut Holes, 24
Sour Milk Doughnuts, 23
Eggs
Breakfast Lasagna, 15
Corn and Wild Onions, 126
Deviled Egg Balls, 56
Huevos Rancheros, 133
Lightened-up Eggnog, 157
Linda's Breakfast Casserole, 13
Mini Egg Casseroles, 17
Panhandle Casserole, 14
Tangy Lemon Curd, 26
Thai Omelet, 143
Wild Onions and Eggs, 127
Working Man's Quiche, 16

Fish
Baked Salmon with Shrimp in a White Wine Cream Sauce, 123
Classic Fried Catfish, 124
Fish Fillets over Zesty Lemon Rice, 123
French Toast
Baked French Toast, 22
Hardeman Guest House Caramel French Toast, 23
Frozen
Candy Bar Ice Cream, 177
Frozen Peanut Butter Pie, 171
Jan's Summertime Peach Milkshake, 157
Lemon-Orange Ice Cream, 179
Strawberry Milkshake, 156
Strawberry Yum-Yum, 181
Watermelon Frosted, 154
Gelatin
Dee's Cranberry Salad, 85
Double Orange Gelatin Salad, 79
Gelatin Pretzel Salad, 85
Ginger Pear Mold, 86
Grandma's Corned Beef Salad, 82
Raw Cranberry Relish, 86
Grapefruit
Citrus-Coconut Squares, 164
Citrus Marmalade, 26
Grilled
Asparagus Summer Salad, 77
Beef Kabobs, 114
Ginger-Honey Pork Tenderloin, 117
Grilled Corn, Avocado, and Tomato Salad with Honey-Lime Dressing, 80
Honey BBQ Chicken, 122
Oklahoma Barbequed Spareribs, 113
Ham
Ham and Cheese Ball, 50
Ham and Mushroom Casserole, 131
Ham 'n' Beans, 91
Jambalaya, 124
Sausage and Ham Jambalaya, 125
Honey
Ginger-Honey Pork Tenderloin, 117
Grilled Corn, Avocado, and Tomato Salad with Honey-Lime Dressing, 80
Honey and Cinnamon Cold Remedy, 150
Honey BBQ Chicken, 122
Honey Poppy Seed Biscuits, 42
Ice Cream
Candy Bar Ice Cream, 177
Jan's Summertime Peach Milkshake, 157
Lemon-Orange Ice Cream, 179
Strawberry Milkshake, 156
Watermelon Frosted, 154
Italian
Chicken Spaghetti, 106
Easy Lasagna, 108
Four-Cheese Pasta Florentine, 105
Grandma's Meatballs, 111
Linguine with Tomatoes, Anchovies, and Capers, 108
Mark's Favorite Upside-Down Pizza, 109
White Lasagna, 106
Jellies
Citrus Marmalade, 26
Corn Cob Jelly, 27
Sand Plum Jelly, 25
Lasagna
Breakfast Lasagna, 15
Crescent Dinner Roll Lasagna, 107
Easy Lasagna, 108
White Lasagna, 106
Lemon
Citrus-Coconut Squares, 164
Citrus Marmalade, 26
Citrus Nut Bread, 32
Fish Fillets over Zesty Lemon Rice, 123
Lemon Bars, 162
Lemon Cake, 174
Lemon Chicken, 118
Lemon-Orange Ice Cream, 179
Lemon Pound Cake, 173
Lemon Wrinkles, 163
Lemony Orzo Salad, 87
Mama's Hot Lemonade, 149
Strawberry-Lemon Slush, 153
Tangy Lemon Curd, 26
Watermelon Lemonade, 154
Meatballs
Grandma's Meatballs, 111
Nana Lou's Meatballs, 49
Sweet and Spicy Meatballs, 50
Tangy Meatballs, 49
Meatloaf
Bacon-Cheeseburger Meatloaf, 110
Favorite Meatloaf, 110
Mexican
Angela's Tamale Soup, 66
Betty Moe's Mexican Chicken Casserole, 129
Chicken Tostadas, 135
Coconut-Orange Chicken Fajitas, 135
Daddy Jim's Taco Soup, 66
Huevos Rancheros, 133
Jo's Beef Empanadas, 136
Mexi-Chili Casserole, 128
Mexican Brunch Chocolate, 134
Mexican Cornbread, 138
Pseudo-Enchiladas, 128
Slow Cooker Carnitas, 137
Taco Pasta, 109
Tamale Pie, 134
Muffins
Bran Muffins, 45
Cheese Muffins, 44
Sausage Ball Muffins, 42
Mushrooms
Artichoke Chicken and Olives, 119
Asian Chicken Noodle Soup, 64
Beef Kabobs, 114
Brazilian Stroganoff, 136
Ham and Mushroom Casserole, 131
Hearts 'n' Caps, 98
Josh's Chili, 70
Mark's Favorite Upside-Down Pizza, 109
Savory Fresh Mushrooms, 98
Slow-cooked Cube Steak with Gravy, 113
Working Man's Quiche, 16
Native American
Baked Indian Pudding, 178
Bean Bread, 30
Corn and Wild Onions, 126
Fried Hominy, 92
Fried Indian Bread, 34
Grape Dumplings, 179
Tanshpashofa, 131
Wild Onions and Eggs, 127

Oatmeal
- Grandma Grof's Oatmeal Cookies, 165
- Grandpa Veith's Oatmeal Bread, 33

Orange
- Asian-style Orange Pork, 141
- Citrus-Coconut Squares, 164
- Citrus Marmalade, 26
- Citrus Nut Bread, 32
- Coconut-Orange Chicken Fajitas, 135
- Cranberry-Orange Bread, 30
- Double Orange Gelatin Salad, 79
- Fresh Orange Salsa, 47
- Lemon-Orange Ice Cream, 179
- Orange Bread, 33
- Raw Cranberry Relish, 86
- Slow Cooker Carnitas, 137

Pancakes
- Prairie Pancakes, 20

Pasta
- Asian Chicken Noodle Soup, 64
- Cheesy Chili Mac, 130
- Chicken Spaghetti, 106
- Company Casserole, 126
- Creamy Broccoli Orzo Soup, 63
- Easy Lasagna, 108
- Four-Cheese Pasta Florentine, 105
- Ham and Mushroom Casserole, 131
- King Ranch Chicken Mac and Cheese, 89
- Lemony Orzo Salad, 87
- Linguine with Tomatoes, Anchovies, and Capers, 108
- Ola Manns' Mac and Cheese, 89
- Pasta with Sausage and Peppers, 105
- Slow Cooker Chicken Noodle Soup, 63
- Taco Pasta, 109
- White Lasagna, 106

Pastries
- Cream Cheese Kolaches, 142
- Flaky Pie Crust, 171

Peaches
- Jan's Summertime Peach Milkshake, 157

Peanuts
- Cream of Peanut Soup, 75
- Frozen Peanut Butter Pie, 171
- Kay's Microwave Peanut Brittle, 159
- Peanut Butter Fudge, 160

Pears
- Cheesy Pear Nut Bread, 31
- Ginger Pear Mold, 86
- Raw Cranberry Relish, 86

Peas
- 24-Hour Layer Salad, 80
- Chicken and Veggie Salad, 81
- Cowboy Caviar, 48
- Mother's Black-eyed Peas, 94
- Oklahoma Caviar, 48
- Pickled Black-eyed Peas, 87

Pecans
- Blue-Ribbon Pumpkin-Pecan Cake, 175
- Carrot Cake, 178
- Cheesy Pear Nut Bread, 31
- Cherry Party Salad, 77
- Chocolate Chip Cheese Ball, 51
- Citrus Nut Bread, 32
- Johnny's Chicken Salad, 78
- Land Run Sweet Biscuits, 39
- Maple Pecan Pie, 170
- Martha Washington Candy Balls, 159
- Mom's Chipmunk Pie, 172
- Multi-Grain Waffles, 20
- Oklahoma Crude Cake, 175
- Pecan Toffee, 161
- Persimmon Date Nut Bread, 37
- Pineapple Delight, 180
- Praline Sweet Potato Casserole, 95
- Ray B's Dip, 54
- Sausage, Squash, and Pecan Casserole, 100
- Shredded Brussels Sprouts with Pecans and Mustard Seeds, 99
- Teriyaki Chicken, 120

Peppers
- Pasta with Sausage and Peppers, 105
- Pickled Peppers, 103
- Roasted Country Vegetables, 97

Persimmons
- Persimmon Date Nut Bread, 37
- Persimmon Pudding, 182

Pies
- Frozen Peanut Butter Pie, 171
- "Here's to the Red, White, and Blue" Pie, 169
- Maple Pecan Pie, 170
- Mom's Chipmunk Pie, 172
- Paper Bag Apple Pie, 168
- Pineapple Chess Pie, 166
- Pineapple Delight, 180
- Sour Cream Apple Pie, 170
- Sour Cream Raisin Pie, 166
- Summer Squash Pie, 168
- Tamale Pie, 134

Pineapple
- Banana-Pineapple Punch, 152
- Banana Split Trifle with Butter-Rum Glaze, 184
- Carrot-Pineapple Cake with Cream Cheese Icing, 177
- Cherry Party Salad, 77
- Dee's Cranberry Salad, 85
- Double Orange Gelatin Salad, 79
- Hidden Veggie Smoothie, 157
- Pineapple Chess Pie, 166
- Pineapple Delight, 180
- Pineapple Spread, 56
- Spiced Cupcakes, 172
- Strawberry-Pineapple Punch, 152

Pork
- Asian-style Orange Pork, 141
- Baked Pork Chops, 118
- Bourbon Franks, 50
- Favorite Meatloaf, 110
- Ginger-Honey Pork Tenderloin, 117
- Ham and Mushroom Casserole, 131
- Ham 'n' Beans, 91
- Mother's Black-eyed Peas, 94
- Oklahoma Barbequed Spareribs, 113
- Slow Cooker Carnitas, 137
- Tanshpashofa, 131
- Thai Omelet, 143

Potatoes
- Cheesy Chicken Chowder, 74
- Corned Beef Hash, 17
- Double-Baked Potato Casserole, 93
- Hash Brown Potato Casserole, 94
- Herbed Onion Scalloped Potatoes, 91

Mini Twice-Baked Potatoes, 58
Parmesan-Rosemary Potatoes, 90
Slow Cooker Beef and Potato Stew, 71
Puddings
Baked Indian Pudding, 178
Persimmon Pudding, 182
Puff Pastry
Baked Brie in Puff Pastry, 59
Tomato-Basil Elephant Ears, 58
Pumpkin
Blue-Ribbon Pumpkin-Pecan Cake, 175
Curried Pumpkin Soup, 68
Pumpkin, White Bean, and Sausage Stew, 71
Spiced Pumpkin Latte, 145
Punch
Banana-Pineapple Punch, 152
Cherry Limeade Punch, 151
Cider Punch, 151
Fruity Punch, 151
Purple-Power Punch, 153
Strawberry-Pineapple Punch, 152
Tangy Party Punch, 153
Raspberries
Individual Pavlovas, 181
Purple-Power Punch, 153
Watermelon Lemonade, 154
Yogurt-Berry Parfait, 25
Ribs
Oklahoma Barbequed Spareribs, 113
River's Bend Short Ribs, 115
Rice
Broccoli Casserole, 101
Fish Fillets over Zesty Lemon Rice, 123
Jambalaya, 124
Lila Clay's Chicken and Rice, 122
Nana Lou's Meatballs, 49
Odie Bob's Chicken and Rice, 122
Sausage and Ham Jambalaya, 125
Sausage and Rice Casserole, 126
Western Casserole, 130
Salads, Fruit
Cherry Party Salad, 77
Dee's Cranberry Salad, 85
Double Orange Gelatin Salad, 79
Gelatin Pretzel Salad, 85
Ginger Pear Mold, 86
Raw Cranberry Relish, 86
Salads, Vegetable
24-Hour Layer Salad, 80
Asparagus Summer Salad, 77
Aunt Florrie's Cornbread Salad, 79
Broccoli-Cranberry Salad, 82
Broccoli Salad, 77
Chicken and Veggie Salad, 81
Chopped Summer Salad, 83
Cowboy Caviar, 48
Delta's Funeral Salad, 85
Grandma's Corned Beef Salad, 82
Grilled Corn, Avocado, and Tomato Salad with Honey-Lime Dressing, 80
Johnny's Chicken Salad, 78
Lemony Orzo Salad, 87
Oklahoma Caviar, 48
Pickled Black-eyed Peas, 87
Stir-fried Beef and Grain Salad, 81
Tomato, Basil, and Fresh Mozzarella Salad, 84
Salsa
Cowboy Caviar, 48
Fresh Orange Salsa, 47
Oklahoma Caviar, 48
Sauces
Caramel Sauce, 146
Chocolate Gravy, 27
Turkey Gravy, 127
Vanilla Syrup, 146
Watermelon Barbeque Sauce, 115
Sausage
Breakfast Lasagna, 15
Crescent Dinner Roll Lasagna, 107
Four-Cheese Pasta Florentine, 105
Josh's Chili, 70
Lentil Soup, 67
Linda's Breakfast Casserole, 13
Mini Egg Casseroles, 17
Panhandle Casserole, 14
Pasta with Sausage and Peppers, 105
Pumpkin, White Bean and Sausage Stew, 71
Sausage and Ham Jambalaya, 125
Sausage and Rice Casserole, 126
Sausage Ball Muffins, 42
Sausage, Squash, and Pecan Casserole, 100
White Queso, 54
Working Man's Quiche, 16
Scones
Cherry Scones, 43
Sour Cream Scones, 42
Sherbet
Cherry Limeade Punch, 151
Double Orange Gelatin Salad, 79
Purple-Power Punch, 153
Strawberry Milkshake, 156
Tangy Party Punch, 153
Watermelon Cooler, 154
Shrimp
Baked Salmon with Shrimp in a White Wine Cream Sauce, 123
Jambalaya, 124
Pad Thai, 142
Slow Cooker
Artichoke Chicken and Olives, 119
Chicken Adobo, 140
Cider Punch, 151
Ham 'n' Beans, 91
Mexican Cornbread, 138
Mulled Cider, 150
Slow-cooked Cube Steak with Gravy, 113
Slow Cooker Beef and Potato Stew, 71
Slow Cooker Carnitas, 137
Slow Cooker Chicken Noodle Soup, 63
Sweet and Spicy Meatballs, 50
Tanshpashofa, 131
White Queso, 54
Soups
Angela's Tamale Soup, 66
Asian Chicken Noodle Soup, 64
Cheesy Chicken Chowder, 74
Chicken-Corn Chowder, 73
Chicken Fiesta Soup, 65
Cream of Peanut Soup, 75
Creamy Broccoli Orzo Soup, 63
Curried Pumpkin Soup, 68
Daddy Jim's Taco Soup, 66
Jill's Favorite Tortilla Soup, 64

Lentil Soup, 67
Nacho Cheese Chowder, 73
Pumpkin, White Bean and Sausage Stew, 71
Slow Cooker Chicken Noodle Soup, 63
Triple Bean Chowder, 72
Spinach
Four-Cheese Pasta Florentine, 105
Hidden Veggie Smoothie, 157
Spicy Spinach Dip, 55
Squash
Roasted Acorn Squash, 99
Sausage, Squash, and Pecan Casserole, 100
Summer Squash Pie, 168
Stews
Pumpkin, White Bean, and Sausage Stew, 71
Slow Cooker Beef and Potato Stew, 71
Strawberries
Asparagus Summer Salad, 77
Banana Split Trifle with Butter-Rum Glaze, 184
Gelatin Pretzel Salad, 85
"Here's to the Red, White, and Blue" Pie, 169
Hidden Veggie Smoothie, 157
Individual Pavlovas, 181
Strawberry-Basil Infused Water, 155
Strawberry-Lemon Slush, 153
Strawberry Milkshake, 156
Strawberry Party Tarts, 185
Strawberry-Pineapple Punch, 152
Strawberry Yum-Yum, 181
Yogurt-Berry Parfait, 25
Sweet Potatoes
Butterscotch Yams, 97
Praline Sweet Potato Casserole, 95
Sweet Potato-Apple Delight, 99
Sweet Potato Biscuits, 40
Tea
Apple Cider Tea, 148
Hot Cranberry Tea, 149
Toast
Cheesy Garlic-Dill Toast, 36
Oklahoma Cheese Toast, 36
Tomatoes
Beef-Stuffed Tomatoes, 116
Grilled Corn, Avocado, and Tomato Salad with Honey-Lime Dressing, 80
Herb-Roasted Tomatoes, 102
Linguine with Tomatoes, Anchovies, and Capers, 108
Tomato, Basil, and Fresh Mozzarella Salad, 84
Tomato-Basil Elephant Ears, 58
Tomato, Onion, and Basil Bruschetta, 61
Turkey
Lentil Soup, 67
Pumpkin, White Bean, and Sausage Stew, 71
Tortilla Roll-ups, 57
Turkey Cranberry Braid, 56
Turkey Gravy, 127
Waffles
Gingerbread Waffles and Whipped Cream, 21
Multi-Grain Waffles, 20
Overnight Belgian Waffles, 21
Watermelon
Watermelon Barbeque Sauce, 115
Watermelon Cooler, 154
Watermelon Frosted, 154
Watermelon Lemonade, 154
Zucchini
Eggplant-Zucchini Ratatouille, 97
Lemony Orzo Salad, 87
Sausage, Squash, and Pecan Casserole, 100
Sliced Zucchini Pickles, 103
Zucchini Bread, 32
Zucchini Patties, 96